I0328832

The Farmer's Wife
A Comedy in Three Acts

by Eden Phillpotts

A Samuel French Acting Edition

New York Hollywood London Toronto
SAMUELFRENCH.COM

Copyright © 1929 by Eden Phillpotts

ALL RIGHTS RESERVED

CAUTION: Professionals and amateurs are hereby warned that *THE FARMER'S WIFE* is subject to a Licensing Fee. It is fully protected under the copyright laws of the United States of America, the British Commonwealth, including Canada, and all other countries of the Copyright Union. All rights, including professional, amateur, motion picture, recitation, lecturing, public reading, radio broadcasting, television and the rights of translation into foreign languages are strictly reserved. In its present form the play is dedicated to the reading public only.

The amateur live stage performance rights to *THE FARMER'S WIFE* are controlled exclusively by Samuel French, Inc., and licensing arrangements and performance licenses must be secured well in advance of presentation. PLEASE NOTE that amateur Licensing Fees are set upon application in accordance with your producing circumstances. When applying for a licensing quotation and a performance license please give us the number of performances intended, dates of production, your seating capacity and admission fee. Licensing Fees are payable one week before the opening performance of the play to Samuel French, Inc., at 45 W. 25th Street, New York, NY 10010.

Licensing Fee of the required amount must be paid whether the play is presented for charity or gain and whether or not admission is charged.

Stock licensing fees quoted upon application to Samuel French, Inc.

For all other rights than those stipulated above, apply to: Samuel French, Inc.

Particular emphasis is laid on the question of amateur or professional readings, permission and terms for which must be secured in writing from Samuel French, Inc.

Copying from this book in whole or in part is strictly forbidden by law, and the right of performance is not transferable.

Whenever the play is produced the following notice must appear on all programs, printing and advertising for the play: "Produced by special arrangement with Samuel French, Inc."

Due authorship credit must be given on all programs, printing and advertising for the play.

No one shall commit or authorize any act or omission by which the copyright of, or the right to copyright, this play may be impaired.

No one shall make any changes in this play for the purpose of production.

Publication of this play does not imply availability for performance. Both amateurs and professionals considering a production are strongly advised in their own interests to apply to Samuel French, Inc., for written permission before starting rehearsals, advertising, or booking a theatre.

No part of this book may be reproduced, stored in a retrieval system, or transmitted in any form, by any means, now known or yet to be invented, including mechanical, electronic, photocopying, recording, videotaping, or otherwise, without the prior written permission of the publisher.

ISBN 978-0-573-60886-5   Printed in U.S.A.   #8015

THE FARMER'S WIFE

Produced at the Birmingham Repertory Theatre on Saturday, November 11th, 1916.

CHARACTERS

SAMUEL SWEETLAND (Master of Applegarth Farm)	*Joseph A Dodd*
HENRY COAKER	*William Armstrong.*
RICHARD COAKER (his Nephew)	*Felix Aylmer*
GEORGE SMERDON	*Noel Shammon*
VALIANT DUNNYBRIG	*Frank Moore*
THE REV SEPTIMUS TUDOR	*Frank D. Clewlow*
DOCTOR RUNDLE	*Alfred J. Brooks*
CHURDLES ASH	*William J. Rea*
MR. GREGSON	*Dennis King.*
TEDDY SMERDON	*William McNiel*
ARAMINTA DENCH	*Mary Raby.*
THIRZA TAPPER	*Cathleen Orford*
PETRONELL SWEETLAND (SAMUEL SWEETLAND'S	*Cecily Byrne*
SIBLEY SWEETLAND daughters)	*Betty Pinchard*
LOUISA WINDEATT	*Margaret Chatwin*
MARY HEARN	*Isabel Thornton*
SARAH SMERDON (the Mother of GEORGE SMERDON)	*Maud Gill*
SUSAN MAINE	*Dorothy Taylor*
SOPHIE SMERDON	*Helena Pickard*
MRS RUNDLE	*Hilda Vane*
HON. MRS TUDOR	*Nancy Staples.*

ACTS I and III take place at Applegarth Farm.
ACT II at the Villa Residence of MISS THIRZA TAPPER.

Produced by A E DRINKWATER.
Music to song in Act II by LAWRENCE HANRAY.

THE FARMER'S WIFE

ACT I

SCENE.—*The house-place of Applegarth Farm in the village of Little Silver. A roomy and spacious kitchen with buff-washed walls, a deep fireplace and range and bright windows with leaded panes and deep embrasures. A dresser stands to the* R. *upon which white and blue crockery is placed Along the high mantelshelf are bright tins and brass candlesticks; above it is a rack with three whips. An easy-chair flanks the hearth, and there are other kitchen chairs disposed in the room. A kitchen table stands between the windows There are doors opening to the* R. *and* L. *The right-hand door is the entrance; the left-hand door communicates with the house, up the steps. An opening is back* R.C. *with door leading to the garden.*

(ARAMINTA DENCH *and* CHURDLES ASH *discovered.* ASH *is standing in front of the fireplace cleaning his gun with an oily rag There is a small bottle of oil on the mantelshelf. He also has a cleaning rod with some oily tow twisted round the end.* ARAMINTA *is sitting at the back of the stage up* R. *under the window mending*)

ASH (*cleaning gun with ramrod*). There's marriage in the air, Araminta Dench, and us that have escaped the state be often quickest to see the fatal signs. (*Puts ramrod on mantel.*)

ARAMINTA. Grapes are sour, Churdles Ash.

ASH (*takes cloth from chair and rubs barrel*). No, no. I've always been very interested in married people since I was fifteen years old, when father kicked me out of doors for trying to show him how to manage mother. Love did ought to be got over early in life. To see an old man in love be worse than seeing him with the whooping-cough.

ARAMINTA. The master's not old and he's not in love

ASH. Why can't he bide a widow man? He's had his dose.

ARAMINTA. He was happy and wants to be happy again.

ASH. How do you know he was happy? Married folks hide the truth for very shame. (*Puts gun on chair*) Marriage don't alter women—(*gets oil-bottle*) nothing alters 'em. They change their clothes—not their claws

ARAMINTA. You talk as if you'd got a scratch or two. Yet

there's something magical in the married state. It have a beautiful side.

ASH (*puts oil on rag*). So have the moon, but there's another side we don't see.

ARAMINTA. That may be beautiful too You'll hear married folk raging and going on sometimes, and saying such cruel bitter things, and threatening to throw the house out of windows ; and you'll think 'tis all over with 'em and the end of their happiness

(ASH *puts oil-bottle on mantelshelf, takes gun and rubs it again.*)

And then, come presently, they bob up again jogging along as peaceful and contented as a pair of ponies

ASH. Yes, marriage breaks 'em in, and breaks their hearts too Holy matrimony's a proper steam-roller for flattening the hope out of man and the joy out of woman

ARAMINTA No, no. Some are built for it Mr Sweetland's the proper pattern of a good husband. He's only got to drop the handkercher, I reckon.

ASH (*rubbing barrel*). No doubt he thinks so. There's no man better pleased with his own cleverness than our man Please God, if he ventures, he'll find one of the mild and gentle sort (*Snaps gun lock.*) We've got enough fireworks here as 'tis (*Puts gun down on armchair.*)

ARAMINTA. Petronell ?

ASH As proud as a turkey-cock, she is !

ARAMINTA. And pretty as a picture. A right to be proud— such a fine thing as her. But she won't be here much longer.

ASH (*cleaning hands with oil rag*). George Smerdon's after her

ARAMINTA And Dicky Coaker—very nice young men both, and they don't live in the public-house, like George Smerdon's brother Tom (*looking at* ASH, *whose head is turned away*) and a good few others.

(ASH *turns slowly round and looks at her.*)

ASH (*moves to table, taps table*). Beer-drinking don't do half the harm of love-making. (*Moves* L. *a bit, rubbing hands.*) For why ? Drink's a matter between a man and himself Love's a matter between a man and a woman and that means the next generation If I was the Government I'd give the drunkards a rest and look after the lovers. (*Throws rag in armchair*)

ARAMINTA Petronell will take Dick, I reckon He'll have Henry Coaker's little farm when the old man drops

ASH (*taking out knife and tobacco*). They haven't got the brains of a sheep-dog between 'em. (*Wiping knife on trouser-leg*)

ARAMINTA. I wouldn't say that. They be both in love, and perfect love casteth out sense—but only for the time being

ASH (*cutting tobacco*) Bah ! It makes me wild to see the men after the women. Poor things—the best of you—compared to us—sly, shifty, and full of craft We be open and honest and straight, and say what we think and mean what we say. The difference between a man and a woman's the difference between a dog and a cat, 'Minta.

ARAMINTA. So 'tis then—a dog can be happy on a chain—a cat's far too fine

ASH (*turning to* L *a bit, rubbing tobacco* L C) Black or white, tabby or tortoiseshell—cats all of ye ! Not tame things, but wild, savage things—pretending to be tame—for what you can get. Marriage is your dreadful business ; you be man-eaters and love-hunters at heart—the pack of you (*Puts in mouth Taking rag from armchair and oil-bottle from mantelpiece*)

ARAMINTA. No woman ever hunted you for love, I reckon—or wanted to eat you, Churdles

ASH Oh yes, they have—plenty of 'em. (*Crosses* R *to dresser and puts the rag and oil-bottle in lower corner cupboard of dresser* R) Them what skim the cream off women keeps bachelors. (*Crosses to* C)

(ARAMINTA *looks out through window, still sitting in the same place*)

To marry be like jumping into a river because you're thirsty. (*Crosses back to fire and takes up hat from armchair—handkerchief to head. Mops same*)

ARAMINTA. Here comes one that never went love-hunting, I'm sure. Miss Thirza Tapper's coming up the garden I wonder what she wants

ASH (*dusting hat with handkerchief*) Something for nothing—according to her custom. Nature don't give nothing for nothing ; why should we ?

(*Knock*)

If she's seeking for favours 'twill be " Miss Dench " ;

(ARAMINTA *puts down her work and goes and opens the door down* R)

if she ain't, she'll just call you 'Minta.

(*Enter* MISS THIRZA TAPPER *door* R. *They shake hands.*)

MISS TAPPER (R C.) Good afternoon, *Miss Dench,* and you, Mr. Ash (*nodding her head to him*)

(*He touches his forehead.*)

This is most fortunate. Where's the family ? (*Moves to back of table.*)

(ARAMINTA *dusts chair back of table at* R *end of same for* MISS TAPPER)

ARAMINTA. Round about somewhere, Miss Tapper.

(MISS TAPPER *sits in chair behind table*)

Ash (*advances to* L C). We've been cutting corn and I've just come for a gun because there's a dozen rabbits in the midst of Nine Acres and they'll bolt presently. Then I shoots 'em. (*Going* L. *Business with gun.*)

Miss Tapper. Wait a moment It's about my little affair—the party, you know. (*Taking off gloves*)

Araminta 'Twill be a grand rally of neighbours, I hear. All the world and his wife have been invited, they say, miss. (*Pulls chair out and sits extreme* R. *of table. There is no constraint about her sitting down to chat with* Miss Tapper. *It must be made clear that there is no difference socially between them.*)

Miss Tapper. Yes—twenty are coming and possibly twenty-three.

Ash (L.C). However will 'e get 'em in the parlour to your villa residence ?

Miss Tapper. There is a french window that gives upon the lawn. Those who have had their refreshments will pass out of the window into the garden to make room for those who have not. And I am here to ask a great personal favour—an immense kindness.

(Ash *looks at* Araminta *and moves down a bit to fireplace.*)

Do you think, dear Miss Dench, that you could come and help Susan Maine with the tea things ? It's the pouring out that will *want* brains. You must keep your head when you are pouring out at a party—so much depends on it. There will be both tea and coffee ; and poor Susan——

(Ash *by fire.*)

Araminta. I'll come and welcome.

Miss Tapper. How good of you ! How like you ! You are the kindest woman in Little Silver—kindness made alive. (*A pause—a little hesitation before asking a favour*) I am going to use my famous Spode tea service—you know, the set that I had when Mrs. Ramsbottom died—with snakes and birds of paradise painted on each plate and cup. It will be safe with you—if you can only stay for the washing-up afterwards. (*She gives a little cry of despair, throwing up her hands*) To hear Susan Maine at work on china—it strains one's religion almost.

Ash (L.). She's my sister's niece, and a very nice young woman. You can't have a shining angel with wings for fifteen pound a year.

Miss Tapper (*abashed, having forgotten this*). No, Mr. Ash ; you can't have " a shining angel with wings " for that money ; but you *can* have as good honourable girl, who respects her mistress's crockery. (*Smilingly.*) And I want you to come, too. I want everything to go off well, but I have had no manservant since my dear father died.

Araminta. I am sure Churdles will lend a hand gladly.

(Ash *throws hat in armchair.*)

Miss Tapper. To borrow a friend's manservant is not derogatory on such an occasion, and I'm sure dear Mr. Sweetland won't mind

Ash (*coming to* L.C.). I'm outdoor man—not indoor servant. I hates they indoor men. I blush for 'em and the lady's maids and all they. Only babbies should be dressed and washed and have their hair done for 'em. To hell with the gowns a woman can't put on for herself! To hell with the men that can't shave their own chins and lace their own boots—that's what I say! (*Bangs gun on floor to emphasize this. Turns to armchair—picks up hat.*)

Miss Tapper. I'm afraid you're a terrible socialist, Mr. Ash. But just for once in a way——

(Ash *puts on hat and stands down* L.C*, back to audience.*)

—to stand at the door and announce the guests.

(Enter Samuel Sweetland, *with pipe and vegetable marrow, up* R C *When* Sweetland *is well into the room,* Araminta *rises and goes back to dresser by window up* R.

Important.—She does this, not as a servant at the entrance of her master, but as now being relieved of the responsibility of doing the honours of the house to a visitor.)

That's quite a man's work, and nobody could do it better, because you know every one of them.

Ash. Better ask the master.

Miss Tapper (*rises, puts chair back a bit*). How do you do, Mr. Sweetland? I'm here begging for favours.

(Sweetland *gives* Araminta *the marrow, which she puts on lower end of dresser.*)

Sweetland (*hanging hat on peg down* R). And granted they are, before you ask them. (*Up to her*) My dear dead partner's best friend won't be refused anything in this house. (*Shakes hands*)

Miss Tapper How good of you! How like you! It is Mr. Ash. May he stand at the door and announce the guests at my little affair next month?

Sweetland (*chuckles, looks at* Ash). He shall come (*Puts pipe in pocket*)

Miss Tapper. And if he might put on livery?

(Ash *turns up Handkerchief business. Blows his nose violently Takes off his hat and leans gun against chair*)

You know my dear father's coachman always did

(Araminta *turns away to hide her laughter and attends to flower-pots at window* R)

ASH (*above chair* L) If you mean that green coat (*above armchair*) with brass buttons as Billy Blades used to wear, I'd be lost in it

(SWEETLAND *looks at* ASH, *and remembering* BLADES, *laughs at the thought of* ASH *in green livery*)

MISS TAPPER A touch will make it fit, Mr Ash. (*Sits again*)
SWEETLAND (R) They be got to the heart of the field, Churdles Best to go if you want a rabbit

(ASH *puts on hat and picks up gun—crosses in front of table and exits* R. *door down stage.* ARAMINTA *takes her work and follows* ASH *off*)

You mean to give a very grand party by all accounts. And I want for you to have a dish of my best red (*sits in chair vacated by* ARAMINTA, *extreme* R *of table*) plums—they Victorias from my cob wall A rare crop this year

ASH (*outside—he whistles and calls*) Come on, Rover!
MISS TAPPER How kind—how generous! Fruit is always such an addition. It adds richness to a table

SWEETLAND. They shall be there We're all coming, of course, and if there's anything I can do to help——

MISS TAPPER. Thank you, thank you. But I have everything arranged. The famous glee singers are coming from Plymouth They will perform under the araucaria after tea is over And I thought perhaps Sibley would give us one of her pretty songs?

SWEETLAND Be sure she will Is young Dick Coaker coming?
MISS TAPPER. He and his uncle, old Henry Coaker, will both be there.

SWEETLAND That's right then For between you and me, Dick has been at Applegarth pretty oft of late. (*Pipe out*)

MISS TAPPER. For a wife?
SWEETLAND. After my Petronell.
MISS TAPPER. She's a very handsome girl

SWEETLAND. Like her father, they tell me. But she's proud —a thought fiery and masterful, you know 'Twill be the grey mare's the better horse when she weds.

MISS TAPPER. I see great changes coming at Applegarth. Your Sibley will soon get a husband too.

SWEETLAND. Sibley's a quiet little go-by-the-ground girl—not so dashing as her sister. But no doubt she'll find her market; she's worth her keep to any man in the dairy alone.

MISS TAPPER. You'll be lonely without them.

SWEETLAND (*rises*) That's for others to decide. (*Looks meaningly at* MISS TAPPER *Crosses to fireplace, stands with his back to it, looks at* MISS TAPPER) 'Twas my dear late partner's dying thought that I should take another in fullness of time Always working for me to the end—always thinking of my comfort. She

Aᴄᴛ I.]   THE FARMER'S WIFE.   11

wandered just at the finish, and the very last words she spoke to 'Minta Dench half a minute afore she died was, "See master's under-pants be put to the fire."

(Mɪss Tᴀᴘᴘᴇʀ *wipes her eyes.*)

She perished with them beautiful words on her lips. And 'Minta's never forgotten 'em.

Mɪss Tᴀᴘᴘᴇʀ (*still seated, wipes her eyes again, shaking her head sadly*). How deeply affecting!

Sᴡᴇᴇᴛʟᴀɴᴅ. Yes—she earned her paradise my Tibby did. (*Pause.*)

(*Enter* Sɪʙʟᴇʏ Sᴡᴇᴇᴛʟᴀɴᴅ *and* Gᴇᴏʀɢᴇ Sᴍᴇʀᴅᴏɴ, ʀ. Sɪʙʟᴇʏ *comes first, waits till* Gᴇᴏʀɢᴇ *is in, then latches door. She goes to* ʀ ᴄ. Gᴇᴏʀɢᴇ *goes to* Sᴡᴇᴇᴛʟᴀɴᴅ, *nodding to* Mɪss Tᴀᴘᴘᴇʀ *as he crosses in front of the table. She nods and smiles at him.*)

Sɪʙʟᴇʏ. Here's George Smerdon, father——

(Mɪss Tᴀᴘᴘᴇʀ *rises.*)

—very wishful to see Petronell.

(Mɪss Tᴀᴘᴘᴇʀ *kisses her.*)

Sᴡᴇᴇᴛʟᴀɴᴅ. How be you, George? (*Shakes hands with* Sᴍᴇʀᴅᴏɴ.) Best seek her, Sibley. I ain't seen her since dinner.

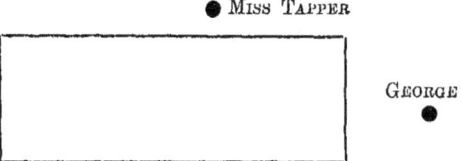

Sɪʙʟᴇʏ (*to* Mɪss Tᴀᴘᴘᴇʀ *up* ʀ ᴄ.) I hope all goes on well for the party, Miss Tapper.

Mɪss Tᴀᴘᴘᴇʀ (*picking up bag and gloves*). Yes, all goes steadily forward, my dear. But there must be no loophole for a failure. You're all coming, (*to* Sɪʙʟᴇʏ) and I know you'll sing if I want you too.

Sɪʙʟᴇʏ. I'm not clever enough to sing before such a lot of people.

Gᴇᴏʀɢᴇ (ʟ ᴄ.). Us be coming in our legions, you'll be glad to hear, Miss Tapper.

(Mɪss Tᴀᴘᴘᴇʀ *moves to* ᴄ. *by* ʀ. *end of table. Chuckle from* Sᴡᴇᴇᴛʟᴀɴᴅ.)

Miss Tapper (*concerned*). I—I only asked four, Mr. Smerdon.

(Sweetland *laughs*.)

Please remind your dear mother that I only asked four. (*To* George, *and shakes hands*.)

(Sibley *goes to door and holds it open*.)

Good-bye—good-bye. (*To* Sweetland, *and shakes hands*)

Sweetland. Good-bye, Miss Tapper—till our next meeting, and I shan't forget the plums.

(Miss Tapper *crosses to door* R , *shaking hands with* Sibley *as she goes out*.)

Seek Petronell, Sib, and bid her come here to George Smerdon.

Sibley. Yes, father.

(*Exit* Sibley R , *closing door*.)

(George *has remained standing, rather awkward and ill-at-ease. He hesitates before speaking*.)

George (L C *by table*). I hope you don't think none the worse of me, Mr. Sweetland ? I be mighty wishful to please you, I'm sure.

Sweetland (L). Why not ? Youth cleaves to youth—'tis nature. I can guess very well what you've come for, George , but I'm afraid—— (*He takes his pipe from his pocket; then takes tobacco-jar from mantelshelf; finds it empty*.)

George I don't trust to myself, you must know. 'Twould be trusting to a broken reed in such a life-and-death matter as this. I don't come empty-handed, Mr. Sweetland. My Uncle Peter's gone and left me a legacy.

Sweetland. Say no more, George. (*Crosses to dresser, leaving tobacco-jar on the table. He takes tin of tobacco from dresser drawer, brings it to table and is* R. *of table*.) These things ain't in my ordering. You can't dictate to childer nowadays—least of all to girl childer. 'Tis they dictate to you 'Twas very different when I was young. (*Sits*) But the rising generation only plays for its own hand, and its own hand don't pat daddy's whiskers no more— (*filling his pipe*) 'tis busy in daddy's pocket. We parents be a necessary nuisance to our children, and that's all. They want everything and give nought back.

(George L.C., *still standing*.)

They say we got 'em, and 'tis our bounden duty to give 'em all the fun of the fair—give, give, give, and expect nothing in return. So whether I'm for you or against you don't matter a button. (*Empties tobacco in jar from tin. Leaving tin and tobacco-jar on* R. *corner of table*)

(George *sits in armchair above fireplace, facing* Sweetland.)

GEORGE. But you wouldn't go so far as to say you was against me? Not when you hear about the legacy?

SWEETLAND. Now take my advice, as a man pretty well thought of for brains, George, and don't name the legacy—not till after. If 'tis even three figures, don't name it. Don't drag in money, for 'tis the last thing that ought to weigh in such a ticklish business as love Just offer man to woman, and put love first.

GEORGE. I dare say that's a very clever thought. To put love first be a great idea. And so I will then.

SWEETLAND. Mind, I don't say love first and the rest nowhere; but I do say love first and money in its proper place—just handy to round the corners, lift the burden and ease the strain.

(*Enter* PETRONELL SWEETLAND *and* SIBLEY SWEETLAND.)

(PETRONELL *comes in first, she has a novel in her hand.* GEORGE *rises.* SWEETLAND *looks from one to the other and smiles.* PETRONELL *speaks as soon as she is inside the room.*)

PETRONELL. Well, George Smerdon, what's the matter with you? (*She goes along front of dresser, drops her novel and sun-bonnet on the upper end of it, then stands for a moment in front of a small mirror hanging on the wall above dresser. She tidies her already perfectly tidy hair, and smiles approval at her own appearance*)

(SIBLEY *pushes marrow up dresser.*)

SWEETLAND. He'll tell you—he'll tell you, Petronell. Give the man time. Don't push him. (*Goes over, takes hat from peg below door*) Come with me, Sibley. How's the corn-stack lifting in the lower croft? It have got to be thatched afore Sunday.

(*Exeunt* MR. SWEETLAND *and* SIBLEY. *He goes out first, smoking his pipe. Door down* R.)

GEORGE. May I sit down here, Petronell? (*Stands twisting his hat.*)

PETRONELL. Certainly—and keep that hat still. (*Puts* C. *chair under table, leaning on back table up* C) What the mischief should you want with me, George?

(GEORGE *sits in armchair by fireplace.*)

GEORGE (*sitting in armchair*). Well may ye ask—well may ye ask! 'Tis a most serious thing, and it can't go on, because it be coming between me and my work.

PETRONELL. All work and no play makes George a *dull* boy. I met your mother yesterday. She told me you'd got a bit of news for me.

GEORGE (*he rises, a little confused, and fidgets, turning his hat by the brim*). A mother would put it like that. You know what pride my mother takes in me—Petronell

PETRONELL. Don't be doing that with your hat. It makes me giddy

GEORGE. I've been so patient as a toad, and you can't say I 'aven't; but now is the accepted time I ain't the (L C) sort of chap to bring red to any girl's cheeks—am I now?

PETRONELL (*good-naturedly—laughing*). Not unless they grew red laughing at you.

GEORGE I'm more likely to grow red afore them than they afore me.

PETRONELL. Don't be such a fool, George.

GEORGE. That's what everybody says to me. But I've got the sense to know I'm a fool, and that's more than some of us have (*Fidgets with hat as he faces* L.)

(PETRONELL *crosses to him, takes his hat away and puts it on right front corner of table* C., *leaving her* C. *in front of table.*)

May I take my coat off?

PETRONELL. Where's your manners? (*Crosses round* R *end of table*)

GEORGE. Don't be so sharp, woman.

(PETRONELL *pulls out chair behind table*)

I won't be spoke to like that I'm here about a thing that only happens once in a lifetime, and ban't used to work in my coat .

PETRONELL (*sitting at table*). Get on then 'Twill be dark afore you've done.

GEORGE. I be coming to it soon enough. A chap have got his feelings. You don't *plump* out a question like this, you creep to it if you're nice-minded

(GEORGE *sits in chair, he takes from up stage, at* L. *end of table*)

Now, I dare say that some men, when they go courting, look for fat on a female—

(*Look from* PETRONELL)

— and a mane of fine hair and such-like outside adornments. And some there be that looks for sense And I be the sort that looks for sense in a girl

PETRONELL. Quite right, George. You'll need it.

GEORGE. Yes; but sense in a girl be as rare as white feathers on a blackbird. And that's why I've took to staring at you of late, with all the power of my eyes

PETRONELL. Your eyes ain't a very speaking pair—I'm afraid, George.

ACT I.] THE FARMER'S WIFE. 15

GEORGE (*gets up, puts chair back a bit up stage, comes down, buttons up his coat, and stands with back to fire*). I'm sorry you think that. But if they didn't tell 'e what I meant to say, more fools them. Now I be coming to it, so don't you miss a word. I've been in a proper uproar about you, Petronell Sweetland, for nigh on six months now—a proper uproar. It don't show outside, but inside here 'tis a burning, fiery furnace; and if I could have trusted myself with pen and ink, like some folks, I'd have done so. But a plough's my tool, and you can't make love with that.

PETRONELL. I didn't know you felt so *deep*, I'm sure.

GEORGE. Deep as a well. My heart be like Daniel's in the lion's den.

PETRONELL Good gracious, George!

GEORGE. True as this hand. And I'll lie awake of a night for an hour at a time and watch the moonlight creep across the floor In fact I'm fair panting for 'e, Petronell; and God's my judge, I'd make such a husband as ain't often seen. And one thing I must say; you could count on my being so faithful as death.

PETRONELL. I'm sure of that, George.

GEORGE (L., *on rug*). Oh yes; and on my money you could also count—every penny of it. I'd hand it over to you with a light heart. You should have the keys of everything.

PETRONELL (*rises, puts chair under table and goes to* R *of table*). Don't say no more about it, George 'Tis quite out of the question. There's a thousand good reasons against; but two will do. I don't love 'e, and I haven't got no use for 'e. I think you're a nice, quiet, honest, good man, and you'll marry a nice, quiet, pretty girl some day; but——

GEORGE (L) No, I shan't—no, I shan't. I shan't marry a nice, quiet, pretty girl I don't want a nice, quiet, pretty girl. I want you. (*Change of tone*) So you needn't go planning the future for me. I won't have that. If you don't take me, then none shall. Be quite clear in your mind there.

PETRONELL. You'll think better of it presently. You stick to work, and save a bit of cash, and forget all about me. You put sense above all else, and though I'm an ugly creature——

GEORGE. I never said that (*Turning quickly to her.*) I've nothing against your looks. (*Quite innocently*) They be quite good enough for me, anyway.

PETRONELL (*laughing, picking up his hat, crossing to* L C.). Thank you, George.

(*She holds out his hat; he, hesitating and awkward, takes his hat. She turns away to* R. *a step*)

GEORGE. But it was your fine brains I was hankering after. (*Coming a step to her*) That's where you shine most in my judgment; and if I ain't going to have 'e, I don't see what's the use of going on living. I—I—oh, Lord, and I counted on it and dreamed on it. (*Turns away to fire.*)

PETRONELL (L.C.). Well, don't cry on it.

GEORGE (L.C., *twisting his hat again*). I ain't crying. I'm only down on my luck. You ought to have took a bit longer to say "no." But there—I guessed how it might be to-day, (*puts on his hat*) for I saw a white rabbit in the rushes last night. Cuss they white rabbits; they always bring bad luck.

PETRONELL. Oh, well, better luck next time. (*Going to* C.)

GEORGE. You say that? (*Follows her a step.*)

PETRONELL (R.C.). Of course I do.

(*She goes in front of table to* R.C., *then up to* L. *of window* R.)

GEORGE. I hope you're right, then. (*Speaking up to* PETRONELL *across table.*) For I ain't going to take "no" for an answer. Don't you think you've done with me yet. I've only just started on you. If I'm a fool, I'll be a fool for something and not know when I'm beat. And there was the *legacy*—

(*Slight movement from* PETRONELL. *She was facing out of window, her head comes round and she is listening.*)

—and all. But what's the money to me now you won't handle it? Dust and ashes, of course. (*Turns away to* L.)

PETRONELL (*up* R., *turns to him*). What legacy?

GEORGE. Sink the darned legacy! (*Turning to* PETRONELL.) I'd have given it all to you, same as Uncle Peter gave it all to me—all he'd got in the world.

PETRONELL. Gave you all? (*Comes a little nearer to* GEORGE.)

GEORGE. All. He didn't like brother Tom, because brother Tom's ways was too lively for him and brother Tom never would stand to work.

PETRONELL. You must have pleased him, George.

GEORGE. Yes—'tis always that way. We can't please them we want to please; but we can delight them that don't matter.

PETRONELL (*at* R. *end of table, up stage* R.C.). How much might it have been, George?

GEORGE. Five thousand pounds—a lot of money they do say. But I'd just as soon it was five thousand toadstools now.

PETRONELL. Five thousand pounds!

GEORGE. Ay! And they want for me to go to Canada—(*the door* R. *is heard to unlatch*)—or some such outlandish place.

(*Enter* SIBLEY SWEETLAND—*hangs up bonnet above door. Gets jar and tin to dresser, takes off coloured cloth.* PETRONELL *remains up* R.C. *near door.*)

No luck, Sibley. I've offered for her and she can't do with me. But 'tis only the first time of axing. If she's going on making my life a burden to me, then I'm going on making her life a burden to her. I'll haunt her, like a ghost from the grave.

SIBLEY (*at table, taking off coloured cloth*). Lor', George !

GEORGE (*crosses to* R.). I'm like that—one of they bulldog fools. Where I fastens on, I hangs on And I be going to hang on till I've pulled her down !

(*Exit* GEORGE SMERDON R)

(SIBLEY *has been following and now puts coloured cloth in dresser drawer.*)

PETRONELL (*goes to dresser and takes up novel, leaning on dresser, thinking aloud to herself*). That simple creature's got five thousand pounds.

(SIBLEY *laughs.*)

(ARAMINTA *taps door* R. *with her foot.* SIBLEY *opens it*)

(*Enter* ARAMINTA DENCH *with tea-tray on which are buttered bread and a big plum cake, teapot, plain bread, dish of cream, spoons, and knives.*)

(*When* ARAMINTA *is in,* SIBLEY *goes out, and comes back in a moment with kettle, which she places on the hob.* ARAMINTA *puts tray temporarily on table at back. Gets tablecloth from dresser drawer and goes to back of table.* SIBLEY *comes from fire to* L. *of table and shakes out cloth and spreads it on table.* ARAMINTA *puts the tray on big table and together they arrange teacups, cake, bread-and-butter for tea.* ARAMINTA *gets five cups and saucers and plates from dresser* SIBLEY *helps set five cups and saucers. Places the two bread-and butter plates, cream and cake, teapot, plates and knives.* ARAMINTA *collects plates and saucers, milk-jug and sugar-basin.*

PETRONELL *has not helped. As soon as the work began she has gone to chair by door up* R., *tilted it back a little, and picked up her novel to read. All is ready,* ARAMINTA *sits back of table,* SIBLEY *on the* L. *side to the front, and then* PETRONELL *takes her place on the* L. *side to the back between* ARAMINTA *and* SIBLEY)

(*When the tea is ready,* PETRONELL, *as she sits at the tea-table.*) George Smerdon have got five thousand pounds, under his Uncle Peter's will, 'Minta.

ARAMINTA. My stars ! He'll be the richest chap in Little Silver.

SIBLEY (*putting tray on table* C. *in position*). Did he really offer for you, Petronell ? That's the sixth, then ?

(ARAMINTA *returns to dresser for remainder of tea things.*)

PETRONELL (*counts on her fingers*). The seventh. Fancy, five thousand pounds ! And no more use to him than it would be to a bird in a bush.

(*Enter* SAMUEL SWEETLAND—*hangs up his hat on lower peg, goes over to fireplace, knocks out his pipe and puts it in his pocket.*)

His wife will have a soft thing.

ARAMINTA (*at table—milk-jug and five cups and sugar-basin*). I ain't so sure. Money often open's a man's eyes, if it don't turn his head.

SIBLEY. It don't mean his happiness, anyway. (*Sitting at table*)

PETRONELL. George Smerdon have come by five thousand pounds, father.

(ARAMINTA *sits, pours out milk, then tea*)

SWEETLAND (*on hearthrug by armchair*). Five——! Good powers! Never!

PETRONELL 'Tis true I had it from his own lips.

SWEETLAND. I told him not to name it—till after.

● ARAMINTA

● PETRONELL

● ASH ● SIBLEY

● SWEETLAND

PETRONELL No more he did

(SWEETLAND *sits in front of the table, his back to audience.*)

(SIBLEY *hands bread-and-butter to* SWEETLAND)

(*Enter* CHURDLES ASH R , *closes door. He brings two empty cider-jars which he puts up* R *corner on rug Hangs up his hat, spits on his hands before taking his seat* R *of table.*)

(ARAMINTA *gives* SWEETLAND *a cup of tea.*)

SWEETLAND (*as* ASH *sits*). Well, well—a Smerdon with money! Wonders will never cease. (*Takes bread-and-butter and eats it.*)

ARAMINTA. A very good young man, and steady as time. And Peter Hawke knew it. (*Pours out the tea and waits on them.*)

(SIBLEY *cuts the cake, a substantial real farm-house cake.* ARAMINTA *and* SIBLEY *do all the helping and passing.* PETRONELL *does nothing beyond perhaps passing a cup; and she herself is generally helped first. When* PETRONELL *tastes her tea, she makes a wry face, and holds out the cup to* ARAMINTA, *who smiles and puts in another lump of sugar. There are two plates of bread-and-butter, one thin, and one moderately thick, from which* ASH *helps himself liberally*)

(*The business of the tea to be done leisurely through the dialogue—not hurried.*)

Ash (*taking knife and wiping it on trouser-leg*). He gave the money to George because he hated his brother Tom. (*Digs knife into piece of thick bread.*) And Tom's in a proper tear about it and George——

(Sibley *bus. with teacup for sugar.*)

(*Cuts a piece off.*) I've just passed him in the lane—and he looked more as if he was going to have a tooth drawn out than get a fortune. (*Eats bread.*)

Sweetland (*eating*). He'll be off, mark me, if you've said " no " to him, Petronell.

Sibley. He didn't seem to feel as if he'd done with Petronell.

Ash (*eating—grunts*). The women will be after him, like cats after cream. Tea, 'Minta.

Petronell. He'll be off to Canada come presently.

(Ash *takes cup of tea handed to him by* Araminta.)

Sweetland. A stubborn fashion of man—so like his father as two peas.

(Ash *stirring his tea*)

Araminta. And proud of it.

Ash (*bus. pouring tea in saucer*). More fool him, and I told him so back along. (*Pours tea in saucer, blows on it and drinks, wipes mouth.*) We ain't put into the world to imitate our fathers. (*Long pause.*) Life ban't writing in a copybook. (*Cup on table With intent*) Go your own way and make history, I told Smerdon not a week agone. Let them follow as can't lead, I said ; (*pours more tea in saucer*) and if you can't break away from your dead father's ideas (*shakes round the tea in saucer*) and your live mother's apron-strings at your age—(*shakes again*) then there's no hope you'll ever set the sieve afire. (*Puts cup on table and drinks tea again with loud sucking noise.*)

Petronell. What did he say ?

(*Pause for bus.* Ash *drinking, holds out hand to keep the others quiet.*
Araminta *moves her cup to other side of her*)

Ash (*bus. Rubs mouth with fingers and shakes tea round in his saucer, drinks again with loud noise—finishing tea*). He said he was quite satisfied with himself, and only hoped somebody else was.

(*Puts cup in saucer and pushes same from him to show he has finished*)

(Petronell *helps herself to cream.*)

Sibley. The people will rob him. He don't know the meaning of money.

Ash (*cutting bread and eating*). Of course he don't. He'll go on touching his hat to a carriage and pair to his dying day.

SWEETLAND. You'd better set your cap at him, Sibley. 'Tis well known if a maid refuses a man, he often falls back on her sister.

(ASH *takes bread from plate and puts it in his pocket.*)

PETRONELL He don't want good looks. Sense is what he's after—sense for his money.

(ASH *takes up a piece of bread and rises.*)

(*Sneeringly*) That's why he came to a plain, homely creature like me.

(ARAMINTA *shakes her head and disagrees with* PETRONELL.)

SWEETLAND (*handing cup*). More tea, and not so much milk, 'Minta.

(ARAMINTA *puts cup on tray, pours out and gives cup to* SWEETLAND.)

ASH (*leaving table, takes hat from peg down* R., *coming to* SWEETLAND). And you'd best to send two *more* jars of cider to the harvest-field. 'Tis a drouthy evening.

(*Points to* ARAMINTA *with bread and then puts it in his mouth. Crosses up to door* R.C.)

ARAMINTA. I've took two down an hour ago.
ASH (*puts on hat, eats last piece of bread*). They're empty

(*Exit* CHURDLES ASH, *closing door*)

SWEETLAND. Did 'e tell 'em about the tarpaulin, 'Minta? (*Turns chair to face* L.)
ARAMINTA. I told 'em.
SIBLEY (*handing bread-and-butter plate*). Have a bite yourself, 'Minta. Where's your cup?

(ARAMINTA *holds up her cup and drinks.*)

SWEETLAND. Five thousand pounds, George Smerdon! (*Looks at* PETRONELL) 'Tis a good bait on the hook, Petronell.
PETRONELL. I'm not the one to be caught that way, father.

(*During this* ARAMINTA *goes from her place to the fire to fill up the teapot from the kettle of boiling water; returning to table she looks through the window* L)

ARAMINTA. Here's Dick Coaker coming in.

(SWEETLAND *turns in his chair and looks out too.*)

(PETRONELL *jumps up, puts chair against wall and exits up stairs* L.)

SWEETLAND (*pointing at* PETRONELL). Ha—ha—there's one bait will catch 'e.

(*The others turn and look at* PETRONELL *as she goes.*)

ARAMINTA (*at fireplace*). Did 'e see the roses come in her cheeks? (*Crosses at back.*)

(ARAMINTA *puts teapot on tray and gets square tray and starts clearing up from* L.)

SIBLEY (*rising and going* R *a bit*) I'll be off out of the way.
SWEETLAND. You bide here and go to the door. She won't be a minute. (*Rises.*) She's only run to the looking-glass. You— (*he rises and puts chair under table and goes over to fireplace while* SIBLEY *starts to clear up table*)—keep him till she comes down house again. And you be off to cornfield, 'Minta.

(ARAMINTA *nods and starts to put the odd things on tray. A knock at the door.*)

Let him in, Sibley.

(ARAMINTA *has been waiting on everybody and has not finished her own tea.*)

(*To* ARAMINTA.) Take your food to the washhouse and get out of their way.

(*She nods, as she is eating and has her mouth full.*)

(*Exit* SAMUEL SWEETLAND *into house* L *up steps.*)

(SIBLEY *opens the door* R. *and lets in* RICHARD COAKER)

RICHARD. Can I come in?
SIBLEY. Of course, Richard. How be you, then?

(*Goes behind table* C.)

(SIBLEY *clears a place, brushing off crumbs* R. *end of table.*)

RICHARD. Fine—and how's yourself?
SIBLEY. Very clever, thank you.
ARAMINTA Will 'e have a cup of tea, Richard?

(ARAMINTA *gets cup and saucer and plate from the dresser and puts them on tray, crossing behind* SIBLEY. SIBLEY *back of table to pour tea for* RICHARD, *places plate and knife for him*)

RICHARD (*very pleased*). If 'tis all the same to you, Miss Dench. (*Closes door, hangs up hat down* R. *and goes to front of dresser.*)
ARAMINTA. I'll come back along presently to clear up.

(ARAMINTA *takes up square tray and goes off* R)

(RICHARD *crosses down and opens door for her and shuts it after her. There is a lengthy silence. He looks at* SIBLEY *standing by door, then comes up smiling to* R. *end of table.*)

RICHARD (*scratches head*). A sweaty day—ain't it? (*Sits* R. *end of table.*)

SIBLEY (*sits*). 'Tis hot. (*Behind table* R. *end close to* RICHARD.)

(*Pause.*)

RICHARD. A thunder planet reigning, I reckon.

SIBLEY. Thunder about for certain.

(*Pause.*)

Be the tea to your liking?

(RICHARD, *who has not touched his tea, stirs same, looks at her and doesn't answer, but drinks tea quickly.*)

(*Nervously.*) Be you going to Miss Tapper's spread?

RICHARD. Be you?

SIBLEY. Of course; we're all going.

RICHARD. *She'll* ax you to sing to the party.

SIBLEY (*shaking her head*). There's proper singers coming.

RICHARD (*tenderly*). Your voice is so sweet as a chime of bells, I reckon.

SIBLEY. That's a pretty speech.

RICHARD (*rather shamefaced*). Do you like it?

SIBLEY. Petronell sings far better than me.

RICHARD (*quite sincerely, with a good-natured smile*) You're a liar. (*After a pause, with a change of tone.*) What did the men ought to wear? Market clothes, or Sundays? Uncle Henry says Sunday black.

SIBLEY Why for not go in that brave grey suit you wore to Tavistock revel?

RICHARD. To think now that you marked that! And you was rayed in sky blue with pink frill-de-dille round your neck.

SIBLEY. So I was, then. You have got a memory. We put on our best gowns to please the men and tease the women. But only the women mark 'em most times.

RICHARD. Shall 'e wear it again at the party?

SIBLEY. Of course. But Petronell's got a new dress. White with a gold band and sweet-peas in her hat. She'll be a lovely sight.

RICHARD. No doubt she will. (*Uncomfortable, and making conversation.*) Parson Tudor is to be there and Doctor Rundle. And my old man's going. He haven't been to a party for untold years I don't want him to come, because his company manners belong to the past. But come he will.

SIBLEY. He's a dear old man I love him.

RICHARD. He's all right so long as he keeps his mouth shut. And I'll tell him you love him. (*Pause.*)

SIBLEY (*after pause*). Will you have a bit of cake?

RICHARD Yes—if you'll cut it.

(SIBLEY *gets up, cuts cake She is at the* L. *back corner of table. Hands him a piece.*)

(*Enter* PETRONELL. *She has made herself very smart.* RICHARD *rises*)

PETRONELL My! Is it you? Whatever brings you, Richard? (*She comes back of table to shake hands with* RICHARD, *between* RICHARD *and* SIBLEY.)

(RICHARD, *at the end of table, is facing up stage to* PETRONELL. *While they are shaking hands, he looks away from* PETRONELL *round to* SIBLEY *on his* R. SIBLEY *pushes* C *chair under table.*)

RICHARD. These here legs, Petronell

(*They shake hands*)

SIBLEY. I must run down to the village for father. (*Crosses behind table and takes her sun-bonnet from a peg down* R. *and opens door*)
RICHARD (*to* SIBLEY) Good-bye, then. (*Goes towards door*) And thank you for your company, I'm sure
SIBLEY. And welcome, Richard.

(*Exit* SIBLEY. RICHARD *holds door open watching her off, then closes door slowly*)

(PETRONELL *and* RICHARD *are both standing. A short, awkward pause*)

PETRONELL (*up* L.C.). Don't let me spoil your tea.
RICHARD. I've done. I must be going myself. (*Pause*) Have you heard about George Smerdon? (*Comes up to* R *end of table*)
PETRONELL No, what about him?

(RICHARD *taking packet of cigarettes and matches from pocket*)

RICHARD. All his Uncle Peter's money, and George is a man used to think in sixpences. 'Twill make his brain reel. Why, he couldn't picture a hundred pound—let alone five thousand (*Lights cigarette.*)
PETRONELL. Five thousand! Just fancy! 'Tis a pity a clever man like you didn't have it. (*Crosses and sits on arm of arm-chair above fireplace* L)
RICHARD I shall have plenty some day (*Puts match end in saucer of his cup.*)
PETRONELL And you'll rise to spending it, no doubt
RICHARD (*smoking—shaking his head*) I won't waste and I won't screw. I'll keep in the middle of the road. I will. But a wife's the first thing us thinks about 'Tis wonderful what a lot of difference even small money makes Half a crown a week on a poor

man's wages have meant marriage to thousands. Why, half the coming generation be the result of two-and-six rise, for the fathers.

PETRONELL. You're *such* a clever chap—

(*He smiles, a little flattered.*)

—you think things out.

RICHARD So I do, (*sits R. of table*) and up here to Applegarth there's always such a lot of clever people to talk to.

PETRONELL. That's why you come?

RICHARD Of course. Be your father going to marry again? 'Tis whispered he's looking round. I've seed his hoss tethered outside Widow Windeatt's farm to King's Head, more than once.

PETRONELL. Mrs. Windeatt—the fox-hunter!

RICHARD. And then, again, they say in the village he's always buying penny stamps from the post-mistress. (*Laughs.*)

PETRONELL. That horror, Mary Hearn?

RICHARD (*with a pleasant little laugh*). They say she peeps in the letters sometimes. And then there's Miss Thirza Tapper and her villa residence—she's in the running, too.

PETRONELL. Oh! What will you say next?

RICHARD. 'Twill be one of them, no doubt, or else some other party. (*Pointedly.*) Then you girls won't be wanted no more.

PETRONELL. We must stop here—if nobody asks us to go anywhere else.

RICHARD (*strongly, but chaffingly, with chuckle*) Come, come—you needn't talk like that. How many have axed you a'ready?

PETRONELL. Not the right one

RICHARD. Maybe he's nearer than you guess.

PETRONELL. I never think about marriage.

RICHARD. I do.

PETRONELL (*turns to him quickly*). Do you, Dick?

RICHARD. Yes, faith. 'Tis a thing you ought to put all your intellects into, when you're about it.

PETRONELL. You believe in it?

RICHARD. I do, then If a man have got faith and hope, then let him try his luck If he's faint-hearted and doubtful, let him bide a bachelor.

PETRONELL. Faith and hope first?

RICHARD. And charity afterwards.

(*Slight pause, and just the suggestion of a look round to door R., where* SIBLEY *has gone out. He speaks looking in front of him, not at* PETRONELL.)

But, before all, faith in the female. (*Sincerely, and as if to himself.*) I'd back *my* fancy with my last copper and—and—there's a woman will know it some day. (*Pulls his chair closer to corner of table.*)

PETRONELL. My stars! You're in love, Dick?

RICHARD (*nods his head*). I ban't no more *ashamed* of it than the colour of my hair. Yes, I'm in—tail over head—(*action*)—swimming for dear life, you might say. But I'm keeping my wits. (*He turns facing her. He speaks as to a friend with whom he can talk intimately about his personal affairs.*) I ain't going to *make a fool* of myself. There's a right time and a wrong time.

PETRONELL (*facing front*). A man never knows the right time.

RICHARD. You speak from experience. Of course, 'tis always the wrong time if the woman says "no." There's a good few very proper men have come afore you with their hearts naked—(*with a change of tone*)—and no doubt, to a proud thing like you, 'tis easy to say "no." (*Turning to* R.)

PETRONELL (*rises*). I'm not proud—only self-respecting, Richard. (*Leaning on front of table* C.)

RICHARD (*warningly*). Don't you say "no" too often, however. (*Rising.*) A girl gets a bad name for it; (*chaffingly and still warningly*) and then, afore she knows where she is, 'tis out that she's not for a husband, and she never gets the chance of saying "yes."

PETRONELL. I'll not say "no" to the right one.

RICHARD (*with a pleasant little laugh*) O-o-o-h! I wonder what his name is. (*Leaning on table close to her.*)

PETRONELL (*pauses, looks at him, almost sitting on front of table so that he could take her hand which moves close to his*). Perhaps you know it, Richard.

RICHARD (*not noticing her movement, or looking at her, with a pleasant, good-natured chuckle*). Yes, I reckon I do.

PETRONELL (*as he makes no advance, she goes to armchair above fire, and leans against it*). The men be all after brains they say nowadays.

RICHARD. Don't you believe it. Most men take a woman—like a girl takes a box of chocolates—for the picture on the lid.

PETRONELL. Do they?

RICHARD. Yes, and then, if they don't like what's inside, they——

PETRONELL. I've got no brains, I know that.

RICHARD. Yes, you have. Sibley says you've got the brains of the family. Now I must be gone. (*Places chair under table and puts cigarette end in saucer.*)

PETRONELL. Poor Sibley! (*She goes to* L. *back corner of table.*) Come in the garden and I'll pick you a rose.

RICHARD (*leans over chair, facing up to* PETRONELL. *With feeling*). Be you fond of Sibley?

PETRONELL. Of course I am.

RICHARD (*nods*). Have she any husband feeling about her?

PETRONELL. Well, she's a girl.

RICHARD. That's nothing. (*He gets his hat, goes up* R, *and throws it up and catches it.*) There's lots about that look to be girls to the eye; but they ain't really. They'll never turn into women—no more than a working bee can turn into a queen.

PETRONELL. Like our Araminta—the toiling, moiling sort. Come in the garden and I'll choose you a rose.

RICHARD. I have chosen a rose, for that matter—(*not looking at her*)—a rose without a thorn.

PETRONELL. Red or white, I wonder?

(*Exeunt* PETRONELL *and* RICHARD, *laughing*, R C. *back, closing door*)

(ARAMINTA DENCH *peeps in from the door* R, *then enters. She begins to clear away the tea things and puts them on the tray and looks out of the window and smiles.* SWEETLAND *peeps in at door* L. *He and* ARAMINTA *exchange glances and smile. He enters and looks out of window* L. *back*)

SWEETLAND (*looking from window*) She's giving him a rose, I see.

ARAMINTA. 'Twill happen, no doubt. Belike it has happened. (*Puts tray in back table up* C.)

SWEETLAND (*moves chair to clear decks for action. Comes to fireplace—stands with back to it*). I must take time by the forelock myself, 'Minta, else I'll be a lonely man in a minute. There's no harm in being fore-handed—eh?

ARAMINTA. 'Tis a wise man's place to be. (*Still watching at window up* L.)

SWEETLAND How long have my Tibby been gathered home?

ARAMINTA (*comes to table, folding white tablecloth*). Two years and a month. (*Puts it on tray*)

SWEETLAND. 'Twas her dying gasp, you may say, that I should take another, though she didn't name no names.

ARAMINTA (*crosses and puts jug from under dresser to keep door* R *open and goes and gets tray*). Too clever for that, poor dear.

SWEETLAND. But we be up against it now. (*She has put all the things on the tray She takes tray towards* R) Set down that tray and help me.

(*She takes tray off into back kitchen and comes back in a moment. Meantime* SWEETLAND *looks in front of him, thinking hard.*)

There's no more understanding woman than you, when you like. Us will run over the possibles and impossibles, 'Minta.

(ARAMINTA *puts jug back, closes door*)

There's a female or two be *floating* round my mind, like the smell of Sunday dinner.

(ARAMINTA *gets coloured cloth from drawer*)

Of course, the first I offer for might say "no"

ARAMINTA (*putting on coloured cloth*). 'Tis any odds she won't.

Women mostly know they're born, I believe, though men often do not. *You'll be married afore the daffodils come.*

SWEETLAND. The daffodils! I ban't going to wait for the daffodils, and me up home five-and-fifty. I'll be married afore the Christmas bills fall in. (*Crosses to dresser and gets pad and pencil from drawer.*) Are you ready? Now the widow man often turns to widows, 'Minta.

ARAMINTA (*sits C. back of table, and* SWEETLAND *places pad and pencil before her*). And seldom in vain, I believe.

SWEETLAND (*comes L, standing by armchair*). I haven't got no special feeling against a *maiden*, however, if she be of seasonable age and not too far gone. Be that as it will, you can begin with a widow. Set down Louisa Windeatt.

ARAMINTA. Oh, I thought so. Clever man.

SWEETLAND. Strong, hearty, healthy, well-preserved. A thought too fond of fox-hunting, perhaps. What's her age?

ARAMINTA. Fifty, I reckon.

SWEETLAND Her back view's not a day more than *thirty*.

ARAMINTA. You'll live with her front view, however. She's a lucky woman.

SWEETLAND (L.C.). She'll do very nice. (*Sitting in armchair which he has pulled to below table.*) Then for second string, let's say Nelly Gurney to Dunston Mill.

ARAMINTA. Don't you do that, Sweetland; she's got a very driving nature and be terrible hard to please.

SWEETLAND. She's always *busy*.

ARAMINTA. Always too busy. That woman wouldn't leave anything for Providence to do if she could help it.

SWEETLAND. Providence have always got to be tidying up after some women.

ARAMINTA. Nelly Gurney's a deal board with a conscience, and a tongue—to say it kindly.

SWEETLAND. I don't want to marry a deal board—nor yet a tongue, neither Leave her out then, and set down Mary Hearn at the Post Office.

ARAMINTA. Not too young for 'e?

SWEETLAND. She ain't so young as she'd have us think

ARAMINTA. A very clever woman at figures.

SWEETLAND. And a very fine figure herself. I like they pillowy women—so long as they're pillowy in the proper places.

ARAMINTA. A woman that's a pillow at thirty be often a whole feather bed ten year later. You don't mind her nature? She's very excitable.

SWEETLAND. Not with me. I'd soon cure that. If I can't manage a woman . . . Set her down third. For Number Two I'll have a dash at Thirza Tapper. She was my Tibby's dearest woman friend on earth. And a lady born, too.

ARAMINTA (*doubtfully*). You don't think she's too far into the spinster state? There's old maid writ on every curl of her, to my eyes.

SWEETLAND. She's well-to-do and knows what's due to herself, and so nice in her ways as a bantam hen.

ARAMINTA. Her villa residence be her god, you know. Some, like her, let their hearts go out to cats and dogs or a parrot; but she's got her villa. I can't see her torn out of her villa.

SWEETLAND. Surely she wouldn't set her little house higher than Applegarth Farm? She wouldn't put bricks and mortar above a fine man's living clay?

ARAMINTA. She might—especially since she built on the bathroom. It's woke a lot of spiritual pride in her, that bathroom.

SWEETLAND. Put her second, however.

ARAMINTA. That's Louisa Windeatt, Thirza Tapper, and Mary Hearn.

SWEETLAND. Just one more for luck.

ARAMINTA. My dear man, you'll never get to the fourth.

SWEETLAND. No doubt I shan't—(*pointing with his finger to paper*)—all the same, you write down Mercy Bassett.

ARAMINTA. Mercy Bassett! Who's she?

SWEETLAND. Her that lives with her married daughter at Dawlish, and keeps "The Ring o' Bells" public-house.

ARAMINTA (*writing*). I don't know her.

SWEETLAND. A publican's widow, and thinks the world of me.

(ARAMINTA *tears off paper and gives it to* SWEETLAND.)

(*Takes paper, gets up, and goes to fireplace; stands with his back to it and looks at paper.*) So there 'tis. Why, 'tis almost indecent to see 'em all on one bit of paper, like they foreign heathen that keeps as many wives as we have eggs for breakfast.

ARAMINTA. But you don't want 'em all

SWEETLAND. No, no—only one. And if my dear dead Tibby was here, she'd be the first to urge me on—wouldn't she?

ARAMINTA. Not if she was here, Sweetland; not if she was here, but where she is—no doubt. (*She gets up and puts pencil and pad back in dresser drawer. She remains at dresser, putting a thing or two in place for a moment.*)

SWEETLAND (L.C.). Yes—none will be more interested to see how I fare than my Tibby. Well, we can only trust the Lord to do the right thing; we can't make Him. (*Pockets paper, moves forward. By table* C.) D'you know, 'Minta, I've a very good mind to go for Louisa Windeatt to-night! Might just ride up over to King's Head and take her by storm—eh? She likes a plucky man.

ARAMINTA (*coming down from dresser*, R.C.). Shall I put out them mustard-coloured clothes, or the blacks?

SWEETLAND. That's a nice question. Perhaps the blacks, and they new yellow leggings, and—— (*Goes* C., *brushing his leggings.*)

ARAMINTA (*goes up to window* R. *and looks out*). Good powers! Here *is* Widow Windeatt!

SWEETLAND (*a few steps towards window* L. *back*). By Jupiter! There now—what d'you think of that? She's getting off her hoss!

(*Both look out.*)

ARAMINTA. She's come about Polly Reep's character, I reckon.

SWEETLAND (*turns front, slowly*). Like a lamb to the slaughter! What shall I do? Tell me what I shall do, can't 'e?

ARAMINTA. Go at her this very minute! You're just in the temper for it.

SWEETLAND (*excited*). So I will, then. Keep they gals out of the way, and get out of the way yourself. (*Puts* L. *chair under table and pushes armchair back to its correct position.*)

ARAMINTA (*at window*). All right. There's lots of time. She's beckoned Ash to hold her hoss. (*Comes and takes off his coat and tie.*) I'll get you another coat and your blue tie. Blue's your colour.

(*Exit* ARAMINTA *quickly* L.)

SWEETLAND (*very excited, shouting up the stairs*). And fetch a hairbrush, will 'e? (*Goes over to mirror above dresser, looks at himself, then gulps down drink of milk from jug on dresser, then looks out of window* R *and goes* L. *by armchair. Calling up the stairs.*) Be quick, woman She's coming

(*Enter* ARAMINTA DENCH, *panting. She carries a black coat, a blue tie and a hairbrush, which she puts on table She gets him into his coat, puts on his tie from* R. *He holds his coat collar back.*)

ARAMINTA. Be your hands clean?

SWEETLAND (*looking at them*). They'll do.

ARAMINTA (*going to mantelshelf in front of armchair and taking a little silver box from it*). And here's your throat lozenges—you'll want 'em. (*Brushing his hair.*)

SWEETLAND (*going to door* R C. *back*). Clear out—clear out quick! Don't mess about.

ARAMINTA (*going up steps to door* L.). Keep calm afore all things, and let her feel you're master.

(LOUISA *knocks on door outside.*)

(ARAMINTA *goes off* L. *as* SWEETLAND *opens the door* R.C. *back.*)

SWEETLAND (*bright, pleased to see her*). Why, here's a brave sight! Walk in, ma'am—walk in. (*Shakes hands.*)

(*Enter* Louisa Windeatt *in short riding habit. She wears a hard hat and carries a riding-crop.*)

Your visits be like the angels'—few and far between.

(Sweetland *closes the door.*)

Louisa. And no less welcome, I hope? (*Crosses to fireplace.*)

Sweetland. Welcome as the spring rain. (*Goes* L.) 'Tis a very curious freak of nature, you may say; but I was actually coming up to see you this evening.

Louisa (*on rug*). Were you? What a pity I didn't know it. (*Handkerchief bus., fanning herself.*) My! 'Tis hot! A thunderstorm's brewing.

Sweetland. And nearer than you think for, perhaps. Sit down.

(*He places armchair nearer table.*)

Will 'e drink? You look a bit dewy. (*Crosses towards dresser and comes down* R. *to front of table.*)

Louisa. No—no—no drinks between meals. I'm putting on flesh too fast as 'tis. Thank goodness cub-hunting's in sight. (*Sits in armchair.*)

Sweetland. And a few brave litters round about, I hear. Now, what's your business? Then I'll tell you mine.

Louisa. I want your dairymaid's character—Polly Reep.

Sweetland. She's all right. 'Minta Dench thinks a lot of her. Only got one fault—she will change her place every year—featherbrained fool.

Louisa. That's not a fault. Servants ought to change every year, in my opinion.

Sweetland. Right—as usual. And now you listen to me. (*He sits on chair in front of table, turning it towards* Louisa.) I was coming up over like the foxes you're so fond of—to pick up a fat hen after dark! Ha-ha! (*Laughing and slapping his thighs.*)

Louisa. We lock up pretty clever. You'd never have got in.

Sweetland. Bolts and bars be vain against a man like me. (*Laughs.*) I'm a tiger when I'm properly roused. "Devil take the hindmost" is my motto.

Louisa. What a man of mystery, to be sure!

Sweetland. I do puzzle the people a bit! I'm that nice in my speech and use fine words. (*Very pleased with himself, leaning towards her.*)

Louisa. No—'tis your funny voice, I believe. (*Laughs.*)

Sweetland (*sits bolt upright in his chair; the smile fades away*). My "funny voice"! You wouldn't hurt my feelings, Louisa?

Louisa. Hurt your feelings, Sweetland! Not likely. Why should I?

SWEETLAND (*offended*). I don't want my voice to sound funny on your ears—far from it.

LOUISA (*frankly*). I'm sorry. I'd sooner pleasure you than most men, and I think you know it. (*Takes gloves off.*)

SWEETLAND. Then don't you interrupt. We lovers are kittle-cattle and must have a loose rein, or there's trouble. I'm like a raging torrent, you may say; and yet there's that in me that won't take "yes" for granted. 'Tis a native modesty, Louisa.

LOUISA. Marrying again? We all knew you would. I am glad. I wish you joy of her, whoever she is. But what's that got to do with breaking into King's Head?

SWEETLAND (*brightly, again quite pleased with himself*). Good Lord, Louisa, you're very near as humble and backward as I am myself.

LOUISA. The fat hen you want—was it for the wedding breakfast?

SWEETLAND. No—for supper. (*Laughs.*) I was talking in parables, my dear. I wasn't only coming to tell you I'm in love. I was going to name the party.

(*She begins to understand what's coming.*)

I've cast my eyes round Little Silver and brought 'em to rest at King's Head.

(*She is getting up. He rises and restrains her movement to rise. Sits again.*)

I've chosen you to sit at my right hand, Louisa. I don't say it in no rash and proud spirit. I'm a man that a little child can lead, but a regiment of soldiers couldn't drive. You're properly fortunate, and so am I—so am I. We've both been married before and both drew a prize. But there's no call to rake up the dust of the dead

LOUISA No, don't do that (*She again moves to get up*)

SWEETLAND (*rises—with movement to restrain her—standing above her chair*) You bide quiet till I've finished, then you can have your say.

(*Crosses and stands* L. *of chair, back to fireplace. She is then on his* R., *but quite clear of him from all parts of the house.*)

There's a good bit of poetry hid in me, and you bring it out something wonderful. Only three nights agone I said to my Petronell, as I looked across the valley—I said, "There's Widow Windeatt's lights a-glimmering up there to King's Head, and here's our lights glimmering down here to Applegarth. Be blessed if us ain't twinkling out for each other, I said, like a couple of glow-worms in a hedge." Pretty good poetry—eh?

LOUISA (*quickly, rather annoyed*). You haven't talked it over with the girls?

SWEETLAND. Certainly not. I'm a secret man. I don't bleat

my affairs. You're the first to know your luck, my dear; and now let me hear mine. Out with it. "*Yes*" be a very short word. (*Brings chair from above, sits and takes her* L. *hand with his* R.)

LOUISA. But there's a shorter. (*Disengaging her hand and rising*) I'm real proud to have pleased you, but I couldn't do it. (*Stands between table and armchair*.)

SWEETLAND (*takes a step back, pauses. Looks at her steadily for a moment. He can't believe he has heard her rightly.*) Couldn't do what?

LOUISA. I couldn't marry you, Sweetland. 'Tis a great honour you offer; but I'm not the sort of woman for you—I'm not, indeed— (*turns, looking at him*) too independent—too fond of my own way.

SWEETLAND (*corner of rug*). Don't let that trouble you. You'll only feel the velvet glove. You'd come to it gradual and never know I was breaking you in. My late wife—my Tibby——

LOUISA. Dear soul! I'm not like her. (*Pulls herself up to her full height and taps her boot with riding-whip.*) I feel terrible sure you wouldn't be able to break me in. If Jonathan Windeatt couldn't, how should a gentle creature like you?

(SWEETLAND *suddenly realizes what she is saying.*)

SWEETLAND. "Gentle"! I'm not gentle. Don't you think I'm one of they poor zanies that go through life praying the people not to hurt them. (*Moves armchair back a bit.*) I come before you in all the dignity of widowhood. (*In front of armchair.*) I come to you for a spouse, not for advice. 'Tis for me to know what sort of woman I want, not you. (*Tapping his chest indignantly.*) I'm not here to ask you to find me a wife, Louisa. I'm here because I've found one. Why have I ridden up your hill forty times since my wife died? (*Pleadingly.*) 'Tis all cut and dried so far as I'm concerned.

LOUISA. It can't be, however. Nothing in the world's so impossible. (*She goes* R.C., *front of table.*)

SWEETLAND (*advancing a step to her*). Do you mean that, or are you only playing about?

LOUISA (R.C., *turning to him*). I do mean it and I'm not playing about. 'Tis much too solemn a subject to play about. I respect you and know you're a good sort, though maybe you take yourself a thought too seriously. But marriage—no. I never felt nothing like that. Some might suit me; but not you. (*Puts gloves on. Bus.*)

(SWEETLAND *is about to speak, changes his mind, turns to* L. *and takes a lozenge out of box, snaps the lid and puts the box back in his pocket.*)

(LOUISA *crosses to him at* L C., *stands in front of him, and holds out her hand. He doesn't take it.*)

(*Quite frankly.*) Good-bye, and thank you for the great compliment you've paid me.

SWEETLAND. If I say " good-bye " I mean " good-bye." (*Turning to fire.*) Mind that! (*Swinging round to her.*) Don't think I shall come up your darned hill again as long as I live, because I shall not. (*Laugh*)

LOUISA (*goes* R. *to end of table, turning up to* C.). I hope you won't take it in that spirit, I'm sure.

SWEETLAND. Oh yes, I shall. I've got my pride. (*Facing away from her.*)

LOUISA (*moves to back of table*). So I see.

SWEETLAND (*goes up to* L. *end of table*). And I'll say one word; you haven't treated me in a very ladylike spirit over this job. You ain't nice-minded—no, you ain't, Louisa. However, I don't want to judge you! I've got something better to do. (*With a wave of his hand.*)

LOUISA (*smiling, but very sincere*). At least we can part friends. (*Again offering her hand.*)

SWEETLAND. Friendship! What do you know about friendship? (*A moment's pause.*) 'Tis Farmer Dunnybrig, no doubt, that have dazzled you; but mark my words——

LOUISA. You needn't drag him in.

SWEETLAND. You'll soon wish your cake was dough again if you take that man.

(LOUISA *moves up stage to door* R.C.)

And one more thing:

(LOUISA *stops at door, facing* R.)

never you let this day's work go no farther. Not to man, woman, or child. I order it. I command it.

LOUISA (*turning to* SWEETLAND). Be quite sure I shan't—not a syllable to a soul.

SWEETLAND (*comes down*). Then I'll wish you " good-bye," (*sits in armchair*) and I'll wish you more sense at the same time.

LOUISA. I'll try and be wiser. (*Going through door.*)

SWEETLAND. And don't you write to me and say you've changed your mind, Louisa; it's all over now. (*Waves her away.*) I won't hear it, I don't want 'e now. (*Quite definitely.*)

LOUISA (*turns, standing in doorway*). I promise faithfully I won't change my mind. I quite understand that this is final.

SWEETLAND. You've brought your doom on yourself—

(LOUISA *turns to go.*)

—always remember that.

LOUISA. I know I have. (*Raises latch*) And—Polly Reep's all right?

SWEETLAND (*jumps up, bellowing it; very strong*). Be damned to Polly Reep!

(*Exit* LOUISA WINDEATT *quickly* R.C. *back, laughing, closing door.*)

(SWEETLAND, *after a moment, looks round as if doubting she has really gone. Then he goes up and looks out of window* R. *back. Then he comes slowly to chair behind table, looking for a moment blankly in front of him. Then he comes* C. *by* L., *takes out paper and reads it, puts paper on table, and scratches off* LOUISA'S *name. Pause before* ARAMINTA'S *entrance. He looks round and quickly puts paper into his waistcoat pocket, and goes* L. *of table by armchair.*)

(ARAMINTA DENCH *peeps in at top of stairs* L. *Then she enters, bringing his working coat with her.*)

ARAMINTA Will 'e change again?

(SWEETLAND *tears off coat and flings it in armchair, and the tie with it.* ARAMINTA *sees that he is agitated and does not speak She helps him into his old coat and takes away the black coat and blue tie. When* SWEETLAND *is ready, he coughs as cue for entrance of* PETRONELL *and* SIBLEY.)

(*Exit* ARAMINTA L. *door.*)

(*As she goes,* PETRONELL SWEETLAND *and* SIBLEY SWEETLAND *enter by the door* R. PETRONELL *comes in first and goes up* C.)

PETRONELL. What did Widow Windeatt want, father? (C., *leaning on table at back.*)

SIBLEY (*comes in front to* L. *corner of table*) Was it Polly Reep's character?

(*Enter* CHURDLES ASH R. *He carries gun and a couple of rabbits.*)

SWEETLAND (*by fireplace*) Damn Polly Reep!

(*An explosion. Pause All turn and look at him.*)

I say—I be sick of Polly Reep

(*They show astonishment. He walks up and down on mat by fireplace.*)

ASH Where's 'Minta to?

(*Enter* ARAMINTA DENCH *up* L)

More cider—more cider! We be all parched with thirst. (*Puts gun by dresser, hangs up hat.*)

ARAMINTA. I'll be there in a minute.

(ARAMINTA *goes behind* SWEETLAND, *and behind table to dresser and gets a large meat-dish, with a look at* SWEETLAND. ASH *is close to door* R.)

SWEETLAND (*takes a commanding position, back to fireplace to harangue the company Bursting out*). Don't you have nothing to do with that Louisa Windeatt no more, you girls. She's a vulgar, low-bred, coarse creature, and always running after the men. No better than she should be—a fox-hunting old baggage!

(*All express great astonishment.*)

PETRONELL. Father!

(ARAMINTA, *coming down between the dresser and the* R *end of table, who is more amazed than anybody, lets the heavy dish fall and break.*)

SWEETLAND (*glad of any excuse for the outlet of his anger*). What have you done now, you cat-handed fool? 'Tis the end of the world seemingly! Let it come! (*Crosses to* R. *Stops and comes back a step*) Who cares? (*Again moves* R, *bumps into* ASH.) Get out of my way, Churdles Ash—(*at* R, *passing* ASH, *who is above door*) —always messing about indoors instead of at your work!

(*As* SWEETLAND *crosses,* SIBLEY *goes front of table to pick up pieces.* SWEETLAND *thrusts* ASH *aside and storms off* R, *continuing the lines. As he goes off,* PETRONELL *goes to* L. *back of table and stares after her father* ASH *stands aghast and holds up rabbits.* SIBLEY *and* ARAMINTA *pick up the fragments of the big dish*)

CURTAIN.

Positions at Sweetland's exit.

ACT II

SCENE.—MISS TAPPER'S *Villa Residence. A dining-room opening by French windows into the garden. The room is cleaned for the party and the chairs and the sofa are placed against the walls. Across the L side of the room runs a narrow table. It is covered with a white cloth on which is spread an elaborate tea, with crockery, flowers, dishes, and cakes. The French windows are open and reveal a good space of the garden. There is also exit to R. of the room. In the centre of the room stands a three-seated ottoman.*

(ARAMINTA *is behind long table arranging things. She wears black, with a white apron.* MISS TAPPER *is dressed in violet silk.*)

MISS TAPPER (*discovered* C. *behind ottoman. She is very excited, and moves to front of table, also helping to arrange it*) The Spode set is safe with you, Miss Dench. And do keep your eye on Susan, as far as you can. She is already much excited You've made the table most striking.

ARAMINTA (*behind long table up* L). A proper masterpiece 'Twill be a great triumph. And Mr. Sweetland's coming up in a minute with a brave dish of our best red plums.

MISS TAPPER. Kind creature! I wish there were more like him. (*Up to window* C.)

ARAMINTA. You may well say that. I never see nobody good enough to black his boots.

MISS TAPPER. Yes, yes, (*coming down*) and the glee-singers must have their tea before they go; but not before they sing (L C)

(*Enters* CHURDLES ASH R. *in the green livery and brass buttons. The coat, which is far too large, is worn over a pair of black trousers*)

ASH (*comes to* R.C). 'Tis too big yet. (*Bus. with coat, showing his displeasure.*)

MISS TAPPER. Beautiful, beautiful, oh—— (*Crosses to him. Very pleased with the effect, and in an undertone.*) Will you *please* lace up your boots, Mr. Ash?

ASH (*going to ottoman* C.) All right! All right! Plenty of time.

(*Throws cushion from chair* R *on floor, sits and proceeds with lacing*)

(*As she speaks* MISS TAPPER *goes to table to fussily help* ARAMINTA. ARAMINTA *moves down a little.*)

Miss Tapper (*coming* L C) True; but some who drive may come early. (*Turning again to* Ash) Is the front gate open?

Ash No. You don't want all the pigs and geese from the common in your garden, do 'e?

(*Enter* Susan Maine, Miss Tapper's *maid-of-all-work She is dressed in black, with an apron and cap She is excited. To* R C)

Susan (R C.). Please, miss, they pink things be all running about as if they was alive.

Miss Tapper. The ices melting! Tchut! Where have you put them?

(Miss Tapper *hastens off in front of her, with* Susan *behind dejectedly* R., *closing door.*)

Ash (*still sitting, lacing boots*). People didn't ought to give parties if they can't keep their hair on about it. She's like a hen wanting to lay her first egg and can't find no place good enough.

Araminta (*who has been wiping cups, etc. Laughing.*) She's all right, 'tis a flustering thing on such a grand scale.

Ash. Waste! Wicked waste, I call it. This sort of wanton feeding by setting labour against capital. Waste—waste everywhere; and if a table like this could be seen by the men in that monkey-house they call Parliament, no doubt something would be done.

(Araminta *gets tray from side table and puts three cups and saucers on it and puts them all on* C. *table*)

But our turn will come. They laugh loudest that laugh last; and the workers will laugh last. (*Lace breaks. Bus of repairing it with string from pocket as he sucks end of string—and coughs.*)

Araminta. 'Tis treason you talk.

Ash (*lacing boots*). The treason of to-day be the reason of to-morrow.

(*Enter* Susan Maine *crying*, R *to* L.C.)

(Araminta *comes from* L. *end of table to* L.C.)

Araminta. What's the matter, Susan?

(Susan *crosses to* Araminta L.C.)

Susan (L.C.). She'll be the death of me. I didn't know they ices would melt if you looked at 'em (*Apron bus*)

Ash. There won't be no ices where the rich are going.

(Araminta *goes to* Susan *and mothers her.*)

Araminta. Cheer up and wipe your eyes, and do your best.

Susan. She's been going from bad to worse for a month. Fuss

and fret, till you'd think she was going to be hung, instead of giving a party to her friends. And I'm only flesh and blood myself. She's got on my nerves so, that I screeched this morning just because a strange cat looked in the window.

(ASH *has now finished his boot-lacing and gets up* R.C. SUSAN L.C. *a little comforted, but still whimpering.*)

ASH (*spits on hands. Rises*). Give notice—now—(*stepping on cushion as he goes up—stops. Picks up cushion*)—this instant moment; that'll shake her up. (*Shakes cushion.*)

SUSAN (*crosses to* ASH). She ought to have more sense at her time of life.

(ASH *agrees, throws cushion towards chair; it falls on the floor near same.*)

(ARAMINTA *turns up to window.*)

ASH Sense ain't got nothing to do with age, else the world wouldn't be so full of old fools. (*Turns up to window.*)

ARAMINTA (*coming down*). You tell Miss Tapper Mr. Sweetland's here, Susan. He wants to see her particular.

(*Exit* SUSAN R *very disconsolately, closing door.*)

ASH (*comes down*). What's he come for? (*Going* R.) There's time for half a pipe and half a pint yet.

ARAMINTA (*up* C.). Don't you drink till after. You'll need all your wits to name the people.

(*Exit* ASH R., *closing door.*)

(*Enter* SWEETLAND *through French window* C. SWEETLAND *is in holiday attire, with blue tie, mustard-coloured suit and hard hat.*)

SWEETLAND. Where is she? Take these here Victorias, 'Minta; and see you set 'em in the middle of the feast.

(SWEETLAND C. *back,* ARAMINTA *on his* L. *He has basket of plums over his* L. *arm. Hot and a little nervous, he takes handkerchief, a large silk one, in his* R. *hand. Having no hand free,* ARAMINTA *takes off his hat.*)

ARAMINTA (*taking off his hat*). (*He gives the basket to* ARAMINTA *to hold.*) Is this a clever time to come, d'you reckon? She's got the party on her mind a good bit just now.

SWEETLAND. So much the better. I'll take her unawares. You can often rush 'em into a thing. (*He goes to the looking-glass on the wall below door* R.) Let me go to the looking-glass (*Smooths his hair, puts his tie straight, looks round to* ARAMINTA.) Be I all right behind?

ARAMINTA (*she nods approval*). Don't you feel too hopeful, however. (*Puts hat on chair* L. *of window*)

SWEETLAND (*down* R., *his back to* ARAMINTA. *After a general survey of his appearance*). No, no—not after my last dose. I'm here in a very determined spirit, of course; but I'm going to be patient. She's worth a bit of trouble.

ARAMINTA. A good wife's a sword in her husband's hand, they say.

SWEETLAND. And a bad one's a thorn in it.

ARAMINTA. Woman's a mystery, in every walk of life, I believe.

SWEETLAND. A mystery always .. (*Going back to* C, R *of* ARAMINTA, *finishing the nice arrangement of his tie*) And owing to their fatal habit of talking too much—*and thinking too little* . . .

(*Enter* MISS TAPPER R., *who closes door.*)

(SWEETLAND C. MISS TAPPER *on his* R. *He takes plums from* ARAMINTA *and presents them. He cannot in consequence shake hands.*)

Ah, Miss Tapper! Look at these here plums. I've picked the cream of the tree for you.

MISS TAPPER. You kind, generous man!

(ARAMINTA *goes back to table.*)

How beautiful! What wonderful plums! A thousand thanks! They will add quite a touch of colour.

SWEETLAND. You put 'em bang in the middle instead of that vawse of flowers.

MISS TAPPER (*pretending to agree with him*). We must see—we must see. (*She picks up cushion dropped by* ASH, *dusts same and places it in its proper position. Crosses, takes plums and hands them to* ARAMINTA.) Arrange them in a Spode dish, Miss Dench.

(ARAMINTA *takes plums and crosses towards door* R. *and* MISS TAPPER *crosses to table and arranges it.*)

SWEETLAND (*to* ARAMINTA, *as she is crossing in front of him*). And don't hurry back, 'Minta.

(*Exit* ARAMINTA, *closing door* R.)

(SWEETLAND *bus. with lozenge box—snaps lid.*)

MISS TAPPER (*crossing to* C.). You always keep your word. It was good of you. But you mustn't stop now. There are a hundred little finishing touches. (*She goes behind table, round the upper end, and lays out spoons.*)

SWEETLAND. Don't you do no more 'Tis all as perfect as a refreshment-room in a railway station. No idea you'd got such cut glass. (*Comes to upper end of table and a moment later takes a cut-*

glass vase of flowers. Bus.) And now just you list to me for ten minutes, please; and forget all about your blessed party. There's far more important business in the air than your party, Miss Tapper.

Miss Tapper (*arranging spoons*). Not for me, my dear friend.

Sweetland (C., *by table*). Yes, there is—for you. Don't think you're one of they forgotten ones—'cos you ain't. There's love in the air, Thirza.

Miss Tapper (*puts a touch to table as she smiles at him*). Whatever are you talking about?

Sweetland. 'Tis the season of fruits and corn and ripeness, ain't it? Quite as proper a time for love as the spring.

Miss Tapper. Dear me! Hark! (*Comes round end of table.*) Do I hear a galloping horse?

(*Both make movement up towards window* C.)

Louisa Windeatt will be sure to ride.

Sweetland (*looks at her*). Is old Windeatt coming? (*Looking out of window.*)

Miss Tapper. She accepted.

Sweetland (*up* C. *In a loud tone of voice.*) A frivolous fool! (*Changes to his softest tone.*) A woman like you—always full of good works—do properly shine, compared to that feather-headed fox-hunter.

Miss Tapper (*taking cloth, looks at* Sweetland, *smiles sweetly, and polishes the brass urn*). Why compare us? Louisa has a good heart and is full of the milk of human kindness.

Sweetland (C.). Don't you believe it. I know her better than what you do. She dyes her hair, anyway.

Miss Tapper. Surely not! Surely not! (*Blinking her eyes.*)

Sweetland (*up* C.). Yes—and starves her waist of room for vanity!

Miss Tapper (*folding cloth*). To think that you observe such things!

Sweetland (C.). My wife knew her inside out. My Tibby put you above 'em all—high above 'em. "The others are all right, but Thirza's a lady."

(Miss Tapper *at lower end of table, behind it, rearranging vase of flowers on table.*)

(C.). She set you as high as that.

Miss Tapper. I loved dear Tibby! (*Comes round top end of table to front of it and puts cream-jugs, dish of cream towards* L. *end of it.*)

Sweetland (*coming forward a bit*). Well, don't mess about, then. Take a seat and listen to me.

Miss Tapper. I am listening.

Sweetland. Yes—for your baggering party to come.

(Miss Tapper *goes behind by* L. *end and arranges and counts plates.*)

There's heaps of time. You said half after four in the invite. Now you and me have been pretty good friends for twenty year, and my thoughts have been turned a lot to you of late. (*Puts plate of cakes roughly on the cups and saucers.*)

(Miss Tapper, *greatly alarmed, reaches over from behind table, moves a vase, and picks up the dish. She puts it down, almost drops it on the form behind table*)

And if the word may be used without offence on this virgin soil, I love you. (*Bus. at table, knocks over flowers, pushing them towards* Miss Tapper, *who catches them.*) We're old-fashioned people— you and me—but none the worse for that, and——

(Miss Tapper *starts and is torn in half between* Sweetland *and the window. She is trying to listen to two things at once and reveals surprise, nervousness and distraction. Coming round* L. *end of table to* C. *of it.*)

And—and—damn it, Thirza Tapper. Sit down and behave. (*Drops flowers and moves down to ottoman.*) D'you know what's happening? I'm asking you to marry me!

Miss Tapper (*sits on ottoman* C., R. *side of same, half frightened*). Dear—dear Mr. Sweetland! This is—and at such a moment! I'm quite unstrung—my nerves——

(Miss Tapper *rises, makes a movement towards table, then reseats herself*)

Sweetland (*excited,* L *of ottoman, takes a lozenge from his box*). Be calm, and don't try to do two things at once. I want to marry you, and that's all about it. I love you, and I'm ready and willing to *show* it. I ain't out of sight of fifty—yet, and if you wore your hair different and had they curls over your ears instead of on your forehead, you'd pass for forty-five in good daylight. In fact, you've grown old before your time. (*He sits on her* L.) But I want you— badly I want you—and why the mischief not? I'm a man a little child can lead, though a regiment of soldiers couldn't drive. I'd be very proud of you, Thirza, because I admire your character something enormous, and I'd leave no stone unturned to be a good husband. (*Kneels on ottoman, both knees.*) As happy as a pair of middle-aged skylarks we should be. (*Rises He takes her* L. *hand, and leaning towards her almost kneels on his* R. *knee on ground.*)

(*She half gets up, then sits again, he, with the satisfied smile of a man who has made an easy conquest.*)

Miss Tapper. Rise, dear Samuel Sweetland. (*Puts out her* L. *hand*)

Sweetland (*takes her hand*). That's done, then! And well done.

(*Rises with the help of the ottoman, sits on ottoman again, and offers to caress* MISS TAPPER) Give me a kiss.

MISS TAPPER (*rising, putting up her hand to ward him off, moves to* R) I beg you—I beg you! It is a great honour to be singled out—the greatest honour of my life. You are the first man, dear Samuel Sweetland, who has accepted my sex challenge.

(*He rises*)

And this is a proud moment in consequence. (*Going up* R.C., *looking at her father's portrait over door* R *and speaks to it*) I wish that my dear father could have lived to see this day (*coming down*), for he used to say, in his merry nautical way, that men didn't like the cut of my jib. (*Turns to face* SWEETLAND, *who sits on ottoman*.) But you have banished that reproach, and I hope he knows it. I too am wanted by a man—and such a man! A terrific experience —never to be forgotten.

SWEETLAND (*rises, comes towards her. She is now a little* R., *he* R C. *by ottoman*). Well, don't talk so much—come into my arms.

MISS TAPPER. No—I shall never seek the shelter of a man's arms, not even yours, dear Mr. Sweetland. I have long ago decided not to marry; though had I considered such a thing, I could have wished for no kinder husband or handsomer man.

SWEETLAND (R.C., *thrusting his hands in his breeches pockets and staring at her*). Good God A'mighty! (*Crosses* L.C. *and returns* R.C) D'you mean "no"?

MISS TAPPER. Don't talk to me in that tone of voice. I never encouraged you.

SWEETLAND (*crosses to* L.C. *in front*). What's coming over women! They'll be at *famine* prices presently. You'll be sorry for this, (*crosses* R.C.) when your damned party's over and you've got time to see what you've done.

MISS TAPPER (R.). I shall be sorry to have caused a good man pain. (*Speaking in a tone of remote tenderness*.) I shall always feel my heart grow warm when I remember this sacred hour. (*Sniffs and wipes her eyes*.)

SWEETLAND (R.C.). Then why the mischief don't you take me? I want you badly—I do, indeed. You'd have it all your own way. (R.C.)

MISS TAPPER. It couldn't be. I say nothing about marriage; but I have my *work* before me—a thousand things—the Mothers' League—and the South African Drug Fund—the Polynesian Widows—and—*and* my villa residence, and so on. (*Turns to* R. *and arranges cushion on armchair*.)

SWEETLAND. I dare say we could stick up a *bathroom* at my place, if that's all. (*Goes* L.C. *by sofa*.)

MISS TAPPER. That isn't all. (*Goes up* R.) None of these things would stand between us, if I were a marrying woman. But

ACT II.] THE FARMER'S WIFE. 43

I am not—though I shall be proud to my dying day that you thought I was.

SWEETLAND. Churdles Ash be right. (*Up* L) You're all a pack of hen-devils under your skins. (*Crosses to back of ottoman.*) And mind this—though no doubt you'll want to shout it out from top of church tower—you'll do no such thing.

MISS TAPPER. Don't spoil your beautiful proposal. (*Hurt and half in tears.*) Don't be unkind to me. I have good blood in my veins, you have offered your hand in marriage to the daughter of Captain Lindley Morris Tapper of the Merchant Marine. I shall mention this great experience—(*pause—looks from him*)—on my knees, and only on my knees. (*Down* R. *to chair.*)

SWEETLAND. Do nothing of the kind. I won't be messed about in your prayers. (*Goes up and gets hat.*) Forget what I've said. (*Comes down* L. *of ottoman.*)

MISS TAPPER. I shall never, never forget it. (*Sits in chair* R.)

SWEETLAND (*subdued*). Well, I suppose I'd better creep off— (*in front of big table*)—with my tail between my legs, as usual. I shan't come to your party now. (*Puts on hat.*)

MISS TAPPER (*rises*). I beg you to come. Everything will be clouded and my pleasure quite spoiled if you keep away.

SWEETLAND. You don't mean that—you're only pretending. (*Up to window* C.)

(MISS TAPPER *reseats herself He goes through window. When he is well through the window, he stops a moment, takes paper with his* L. *hand from his waistcoat pocket. She is sitting on edge of armchair* R., *almost in tears as he goes out.*)

(*Exit* SWEETLAND, *scratching name off list.*)

(MISS TAPPER, *sitting, stares in front of her. She is a good deal moved. She brings out a pocket handkerchief, wipes her eyes and blows her nose.*)

(*Enter* ARAMINTA DENCH *with the red plums on a dish* R. *She crosses up* C., *looks out of window after* SWEETLAND *before she speaks.*)

ARAMINTA (*sadly*) I see he's gone off with his head down. (*Crosses to table* L., *and places the dish.*)

MISS TAPPER. What a man! What a tower of strength!

(ARAMINTA *sees flowers on floor.*)

What a rare spirit, Miss Dench!

ARAMINTA. You want to live with him to see the beautiful truth of him As kind and as gentle—why, a little child could——

MISS TAPPER. So he said! So he said!

(ARAMINTA *picks up flowers*)

And I wanted all my nerve for my little affair. (*Goes and looks in box on table* R. *by door, returns to* C.) Excuse me, I must get my smelling-salts. I—one never has one's smelling-salts when——

ARAMINTA. Can I get them for you?

(*Enter* SUSAN MAINE *with pile of plates to* R.C.)

MISS TAPPER. I'll get them myself. (*Crosses to* R C.)

(*Exit* MISS TAPPER *after running into* SUSAN *and dodging her, shaking her head and rather unsteady, closing the door.*

ARAMINTA *displays wonder and regret. As near as she thinks she may venture,* ARAMINTA *puts plums in a central prominent position, moving the flower-vase a little behind to do so. A tall vase—a low dish.* SUSAN *goes to behind table at top end, and puts down plates under dish of cakes.*)

SUSAN (*by table* L.). Will you pour the coffee, Miss Dench, please?

ARAMINTA. Yes, I'll do it. I'll do all the pouring. You can carry round the cups. (*Goes behind table and replaces plate from form on table.*)

(*Re-enter* MISS TAPPER *with smelling-salts—goes* L.C., *followed by* CHURDLES ASH R. *with white gloves.*)

ASH (R.C.). The party have begun. Here's the Smerdon wagonette. (*Putting on gloves.*)

MISS TAPPER (L.C.). How many are in it, Churdles Ash? (*Sniffing salts.*)

ASH. Five all told.

MISS TAPPER (L.C.). I said *four* so particularly!

ASH. Old Ben's driving 'em. He ain't coming to the party, is he? (*Spits on gloves.*)

(MISS TAPPER *puts salts on table* C. ASH *goes to the door* R. *and throws it open.* ARAMINTA *and* SUSAN *are behind table.*)

ARAMINTA. Shall we light up now, Miss Tapper?

MISS TAPPER (L.C.). Not yet. They are nearly ten minutes too soon.

ASH (*now stationed at the door*). Mrs. Smerdon, Mr. George Smerdon, Miss Sophie Smerdon, and Master Teddy Smerdon.

(*Enter the* SMERDONS—*a mother and her three children.* MISS SOPHIE *is* 12, MASTER TEDDY 10.)

(MISS TAPPER *shakes hands with* MRS. SMERDON, *and then with the children—she kisses* SOPHIE *and* TEDDY.)

(GEORGE SMERDON *stops, offers to shake hands with* CHURDLES ASH.)

No, no! You mustn't shake hands with me to-day, George. I'm not the party.

(*Exit* ASH R., *closing door.*)

(GEORGE *up* R.C.)

MRS. SMERDON. Good afternoon, Miss Tapper.

MISS TAPPER (*to* MRS. SMERDON). The first to arrive! So glad to see you. Sophie dear! (*Kisses her. Places* SOPHIE *on chair up* R.) And Teddy! (*Kisses him.*) What a man he's growing!

(*The two children, at first rather shy, crowd up awkwardly to their mother.* MRS. SMERDON *takes them up* R.)

MRS. SMERDON (*pushes* TEDDY *roughly to chair by door up* R. SOPHIE *on seat up* R. *next to him.* SOPHIE *sits at first very stiff and prim.*) You've heard tell about George? (*Crosses to sofa* L.)

MISS TAPPER (*shaking hands with* GEORGE SMERDON). I have, indeed!

GEORGE (*behind ottoman*). They be at me to share with brother Tom; but I don't know——

(SOPHIE *and* TEDDY *look at the table and grin at* ARAMINTA *and* SUSAN TEDDY *points out the cakes to* SOPHIE *a little later.*)

MRS. SMERDON (*sitting middle of sofa* L.). What do you think, Miss Tapper? Did George ought to share with his elder brother?

MISS TAPPER. Certainly not. (*She goes to sofa* L.) George's uncle left him the money because he liked him best. *We* must respect the wishes of the dead. (*Sits* R. *of* MRS. SMERDON.)

MRS SMERDON. George is as good as gold—always was; but my Tom has more dash in him. Always after a petticoat, that boy. Nature will shout, Miss Tapper, but, as I've told Tom scores of times, 'tis no good listening to nature on eighteen shillings a week.

(GEORGE *during above speech looks round the room and at portrait and ship.*)

GEORGE (*crossing over to about* R. *of table, to* ARAMINTA) Be the Sweetlands coming, Miss Dench?

ARAMINTA (*nods*). They ordained to come.

(ASH *enters* R.)

ASH (*at door*). Mr. Valiant Dunnybrig.

(*Enter* VALIANT DUNNYBRIG—*a genial man with flowing beard. Exit* ASH, *closing door.*)

(MISS TAPPER *rises and meets* DUNNYBRIG *up* C.)

DUNNYBRIG. Not too soon, I hope? (*Shakes hands with* MISS TAPPER.) How do—how do, all? A very fine day for your party, thank God!—I wish I'd had some like it for saving my corn. My stars, what a brave sight! (*He indicates the table.*)

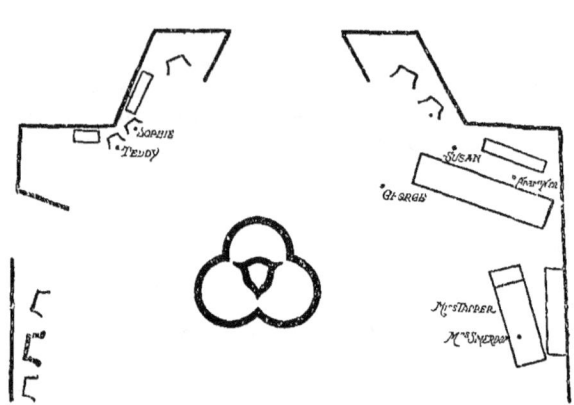

Miss Tapper How do you do, Mr. Dunnybrig?

(Miss Tapper *goes up to* Sophie George *comes down to ottoman*.)

Dunnybrig. Mrs. Smerdon, too! (*Crosses, shakes hands with her. Moving back to* c. *in front of ottoman.*) And George, I see! (*Shakes hands.*) What won't money do! But 'twill take you far higher than this, George, if you only handle it clever.

(*During the above speech* Miss Tapper *takes the children one on each side of her, and points out the picture and ship.*)

George. Did I ought to share it with my brother Tom? (L. *of ottoman*)

Dunnybrig (c). Not a chance!—idle rogue!

(*The children return to their seats up* R.)

(*All now being clear between* Teddy *and the table, he stares at the cakes, etc. He catches* Sophie's *eye, and points* Sophie *looks, too, and she and* Teddy *exchange glances of appreciative wonder.* Susan *sees them and giggles.* Miss Tapper *turns round and looks reprovingly at* Susan. Araminta, *who has seen what the children are doing, and is amused, checks* Susan *with a kindly smile*)

Mrs. Smerdon (*on sofa*). Don't you say that, Valiant Dunnybrig. The boys will sow their wild oats

(Miss Tapper *gets book from table.*)

Dunnybrig. Then let 'em reap their wild oats. George didn't sow no wild oats; no more did I; no more did your husband.

(Miss Tapper *gives book to children and stands* R. *of them.*)

Mrs. Smerdon. 'Tis all character. There's no virtue in not sowing wild oats, if you ain't got none to sow.

(George *sits on* R. *of* Mrs. Smerdon *on sofa.*)

(Miss Tapper *shepherds* Sophie *and* Teddy *and shows them the portrait of the Captain.* Teddy *gets behind her, and stares at the table.*)

Dunnybrig (*going. To* Miss Tapper. *Up* R.). Do you expect Louisa Windeatt of King's Head? (*In front of small table.*)

(Miss Tapper *comes* R.C., *meeting* Dunnybrig. Sophie *and* Teddy *are now left sitting together up* R *They point at the table.*)

Miss Tapper. I do—she promised to come.
Dunnybrig. That's right! She'll put life into it She's worth her corn at a feast or a funeral, that woman. Don't you fear 'twill lag after she comes.

(Miss Tapper *goes into window* C.)

(*To* Araminta, *he crosses to end by table.*) How be you, Miss Dench? Ain't you in the party? I'll warrant there's many coming not half so good as you.

(Araminta *smiles pleasantly, but remembers what she is doing.*)

(*Enter* Churdles Ash R)

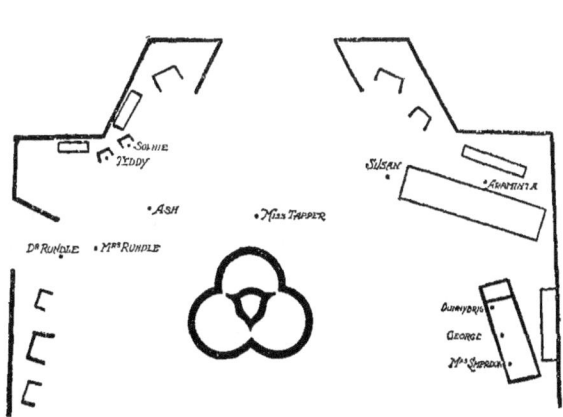

(Mrs Rundle *is just in view at the door.*)
Ash (*announces*). Doctor Rundle and Mrs. Rundle.

(Ash *lets door swing back in* Mrs Rundle's *face. Pause; sees his mistake and then opens it, and motions with head.*)

(Miss Tapper *fussily comes down* c)

(*Enter* Mrs Rundle *and* Dr. Rundle. *Exit* Ash r., *closing door.*)

(Miss Tapper *shakes hands with both.* Dunnybrig *shakes hands with* Mrs. Rundle, *who is* l. *of* Rundle. Rundle *nods to* Dunnybrig, *and sits on her* r. *as soon as* Rundle *has passed.* Dunnybrig *takes* Mrs. Rundle *to sofa* l., *and they sit: he back to audience, she on the* l.)

Miss Tapper. Ah, Mrs. Rundle! Welcome, Doctor! So good of you both to come.

(Teddy *crosses to table.*)

Dr. Rundle. So good of you to ask us. (*Crossing front of ottoman to sofa.*) Ah, Smerdon (*nods to* George, *who rises*), we've all got to congratulate you, I hear. How do, Mrs Smerdon? How are you? (*Shakes hands with* Mrs. Smerdon.)

(Teddy *at table.*)

(Miss Tapper *sits on* r. *of ottoman.*)

Mrs. Smerdon. I'm all right, Doctor, but I wish you'd cast your eye on Teddy. (*Rising.*) Come here, Teddy boy.

(George *goes and sits on gilt chair up* l.c. Dr. Rundle *sits on sofa* l. Mrs. Smerdon *drags* Teddy, *who struggles away from the table up* l.)

He broke out all spotty-faced yesterday, and they be all over his chest, too.

Dr. Rundle (*bus.; motions* Teddy *to put out his tongue, which he does. Trying to look serious, but hardly concealing a smile*). H'm! Too many jam tarts and lollipops.

Teddy (l.c.) N-n-no.

Dr. Rundle (*with a warning finger*). Boys cannot live by brandy-balls alone. This is the dreadful result of spending too many pennies at Mother Pearn's. No more sweets or puddings for a week.

Teddy. I'll begin to-morrow.

Mrs. Smerdon. You'll begin to-day.

(*His mother remonstrates, but* Teddy *grabs cake and is pushed violently, escapes, joins his sister.* Dr. Rundle *laughs and turns to* Dunnybrig. Miss Tapper *rises and crosses to* l c. *of table.*)

(Mrs. Smerdon *having pushed* Teddy *to his chair, bus. with bodice, and goes to ottoman and sits* r.)

Miss Tapper (*to* Araminta). Light up now, please.

ACT II.]   THE FARMER'S WIFE.   49

(ARAMINTA *with box of matches lights the taper that* SUSAN *holds.*
SUSAN *lights lamp.* DUNNYBRIG *rises from back of ottoman.*)

DR. RUNDLE (*to* DUNNYBRIG). You've got your corn in, I see.
DUNNYBRIG (*sits by* DR. RUNDLE *on sofa*). Such as it is—a crop so thin as an old man's hair. Be you ready for that load of hay, Doctor?
DR RUNDLE. Any time—any time!

(CHURDLES ASH *enters* R. *and announces*)

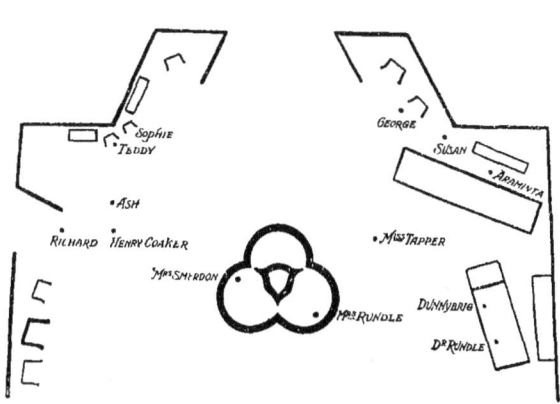

ASH. Mr. Henry Coaker and his nephy, Mr. Richard Coaker.

(*Enter* HENRY COAKER—*a very old man—and* RICHARD COAKER *Exit* ASH R, *closing door*)

(MISS TAPPER *receives them behind ottoman* R.C.)

HENRY. Us be come to the feast, ma'am.
MISS TAPPER (*shakes hands*) And very welcome—very welcome indeed, Mr. Coaker. (*Crosses in front to* RICHARD) And you too, Mr. Richard (*Shakes hands.*)

(RICHARD R C. *with* MISS TAPPER.)

HENRY. There's no parties now like the old ones; but I'm sure you've done your bestest.

(HENRY *goes towards table.* ARAMINTA *and* SUSAN *pour milk into cups.*)

Nothing have been spared, that's sartain.

(RICHARD *and* MISS TAPPER *move up and talk together in window* C.)

D

Ah! and Valiant he invited I see How's yourself, Valiant? (*Goes down* L. *of ottoman, near to* DUNNYBRIG, *who shakes hands with him.*)

(HENRY *and* DR. RUNDLE *exchange nods.*)

DUNNYBRIG. Very clever, my old dear. And you'm pretty pert seemingly
HENRY. I be getting terrible old. I can't let down my food like I did.

(MRS. SMERDON *rises and goes to* SOPHIE, *takes book from her and gives it to* TEDDY; *having touched up* SOPHIE'S *hair, and smoothed her frock, takes her by the hand and brings her down to* MRS RUNDLE. MRS RUNDLE *kisses* SOPHIE, *and* SOPHIE *stands* R. *by* MRS. SMERDON, *who re-seats herself*)

But I be going to have a dash this afternoon.

DUNNYBRIG. Don't you eat they rubbishy things. They'll turn on 'e afterwards.
HENRY When an old man like me tries for a bit o' fun, 'tis like a dog stealing a bone with his eye on the whip.

(MISS TAPPER *crosses* RICHARD *to* R)

Nature's a regular female, Valiant She tempts us on, and then, when we do what she wants, she gives us hell!
DUNNYBRIG (*still seated on sofa*). 'Tis true. She will have her price.
HENRY I shall soon be done with the joys of the flesh now
DUNNYBRIG I shan't I shall never have done with the flesh —while there's any left on my bones, Henry. Ha-ha!

(MISS TAPPER *turns to* TEDDY *and admonishes him*)

HENRY You be a boy still (*Digs* DUNNYBRIG *in ribs, shakes hands with* DR RUNDLE, *and goes up to table*)
RICHARD (*goes to* GEORGE *up* L, *who rises*). Well, George, you don't look as if your money weighed any lighter.
GEORGE (*gets up and speaks to* RICHARD *on his* R.) Did I ought to share it with brother Tom, Richard?
RICHARD. Share it with Tom! You might so soon share it with all the girls in Plymouth right away.

(SOPHIE *nose bus* MRS. SMERDON *wipes it*)

(*Anxiously*). Are the Sweetlands coming?
GEORGE They are
RICHARD I passed Mary Hearn down the road. A flower show's a fool to her.

(*There is constant movement during the scene, and the people walk about in groups, then part and form new groups*)

MISS TAPPER (*turns to them up* R C) May I ask you all to be seated ? It will make more room for the coming guests. Talk to me for a little while, Mr. Coaker. (*Crosses to him up* L C.) I'm sure you want a chair.

HENRY. I do, my dear I be gone so weak in the hams nowadays that——

(TEDDY *puts book back on table* R.C *and sits in chair nearest table* R.C)

(MISS TAPPER *starts and leaves* HENRY, *goes up and speaks to* RICHARD *and* GEORGE C RICHARD *is annoyed with his uncle and* GEORGE *smiling.*)

DR. RUNDLE (*on sofa*). Hush, Uncle! You've frightened Miss Tapper away. You mustn't use that language at an old maid's tea-party.

HENRY (L.C.). Language, Doctor! Me! I'm a very sweet-mouthed old man—ain't I, Valiant ?

DUNNYBRIG (*on sofa*). Never been known to use a crooked word since your wife died, Henry.

HENRY (*going* R.C.). Now, Thirza Tapper's father—the old sea-captain—'twas enough to blast the crops in the field, to hear him when he was worrited When do us draw up to the table, souls ?

DR. RUNDLE (*seated*) We don't draw up. They bring the tea round.

HENRY. "Don't draw up"! What a funny party!

(HENRY *looks round, sees* SOPHIE, *and with a wink to* DR. RUNDLE *and enjoying his joke, creeps up and tickles her bare leg.* SOPHIE *gives a little scream, jumps, turns round, sees* HENRY, *laughs, very pleased at meeting the old man of whom she is clearly very fond, laughs, throws her arm round him and kisses him—then* HENRY *carries her over to armchair down* R. *He sits, rather out of breath with his moment's romp, with* SOPHIE *on his knee, facing audience ; all the others, except* GEORGE *and particularly including* SUSAN, *have laughed at the incident.* SUSAN *places silver kettle and pours water into teapot*)

(CHURDLES ASH *enters* R)

ASH. Mrs. Windeatt from King's Head.

(*Enter* LOUISA WINDEATT R., *and exit* ASH R , *closing door.*)

(MISS TAPPER *crosses to* R.C.)

(DUNNYBRIG *gets up eagerly.*)

(MRS. SMERDON *and* MRS. RUNDLE *go to sofa and sit above* DR. RUNDLE. DUNNYBRIG *meets* LOUISA *just above settee* R.C.)

DUNNYBRIG. At last! (*Hastens to door, getting in front of* MISS TAPPER, *and shakes* LOUISA'S *hand.*)

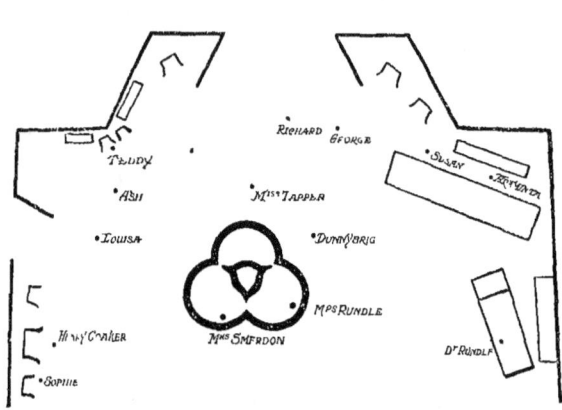

Here you be—neat as ninepence! Now the sun will shine! (*Shakes hands for a long time while* MISS TAPPER *waits to greet* LOUISA WINDEATT)

(GEORGE *sits on chair* L. *by window*—ARAMINTA *pours tea and coffee into cups.*)

LOUISA. Do let go, Mr. Dunnybrig; here's Miss Tapper. How do you do, Thirza?
MISS TAPPER (*comes between them. Shakes hands*). Welcome, dear Louisa—always welcome.

(LOUISA *shakes hands with* RICHARD *and goes down* R. *and greets* HENRY *and* SOPHIE.)

DUNNYBRIG. That's right—a proper good fairy wherever she goes. (*Crosses to* R. *end of table* L.) Shall I fetch her a cup of the best?
MISS TAPPER (C. *above ottoman*). Presently, presently. They'll bring round the tea and coffee presently. (*Crosses to large table*)
DUNNYBRIG (*crosses in front of* MISS TAPPER *to* LOUISA WINDEATT, *who comes to him* R. *of ottoman*) None the worse for that run yester morn?

(SUSAN *puts sugar in a few cups*)

LOUISA. All the better.
DUNNYBRIG. Did 'e kill?
LOUISA. No—we lost him.

Act II.]   THE FARMER'S WIFE.   53

Dunnybrig. I seed you go over a stone wall and my heart went in my mouth.

Louisa. Did you care?

(*Enter* Churdles Ash r., *beckoning to* Miss Tapper.)

Dunnybrig. You know if I cared! (*Takes her hand.*)
Louisa. We're blocking the gangway. Let's sit down.

(Dunnybrig *and* Louisa *sit on ottoman, he at the back of it, she on his* L., *both back to audience; he puts his* L. *arm behind her on top of ottoman and continues to monopolize her.* Richard *calls* Miss Tapper *to go to* Ash, *who crosses to* R.C.)

Ash (R.C. *to* Miss Tapper). Here's a stranger man, and I can't call him out, because I don't know his name!

(*Enter* Mr. Gregson.)

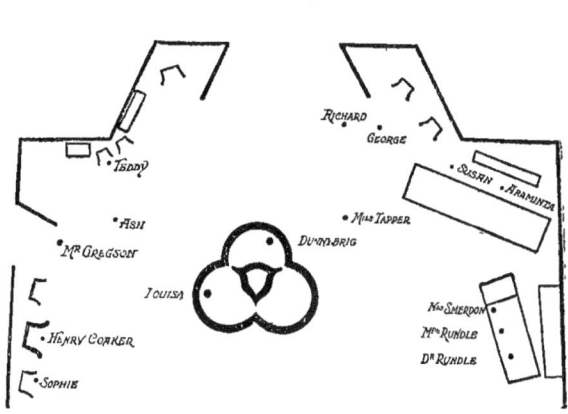

Miss Tapper (*in a half-whisper, with an attempt to hush* Ash). Ask him, then—ask him!

(Susan *fills teapot.* Richard *in window.*)

Ash. Aw! (*Hastens back in time to stop* Mr. Gregson.) Wait—wait! (*Pushing him out again.*) Don't be so pushing. (*Beckons him to come forward—he comes.*) Your name, please?

(Susan *refills teapot.*)

Gregson. Gregson. This is Miss Tapper's party, isn't it?
Ash. Use your eyes.

(Teddy *crosses to big table to get a cake. Noise at cue* "Araucaria.")

ASH (*to* MISS TAPPER *in a loud whisper*). Gregson, his name be.

(MISS TAPPER *crosses to him.* ASH C. *behind ottoman* C.)

MISS TAPPER (R.C.). Ah, the Glee Singers!

(RICHARD *goes* R.C. *by small table.*)

GREGSON (R C , *coming forward to* R.C.) We have arrived, madam.

(*Second* GLEE SINGER *follows behind him.*)

MISS TAPPER. You sing in the garden—where the chairs are arranged under the araucaria

(TEDDY *has got behind them over to table and made a raid, securing cakes. His mother comes to him, and there is a scuffle* MRS. SMERDON *endeavouring to place him across her knee and spank him.* L. *side of ottoman*)

TEDDY. I want some! I want some!
MISS TAPPER. Mr. Ash, will you please take him into the garden?
TEDDY. I don't want to go into the garden.
MISS TAPPER. And show him the little rabbits.
ASH (C.). I will He can't eat them.
TEDDY. I don't want to see the rabbits.

(*Bus.* SOPHIE *and* HENRY.)

(ASH *picks up* TEDDY *and takes him off* C. *to* R., *followed by* MRS. SMERDON)

MISS TAPPER (R.C. *to* GREGSON). Kindly follow me.

(*Exit* MISS TAPPER C. *into the garden.* MR. GREGSON *and three singers go out after her.*)

(*After exit* HENRY *puts* SOPHIE *on chair down* R., *gives her his stick, which she places on floor.* SUSAN *crosses with cups of tea for* SOPHIE *and* HENRY.)

(*Re-enter* MRS. SMERDON.)

MRS SMERDON (C *on* GEORGE'S R). Here, George, and you, Dick Coaker, help the maidens with the cakes, and carry 'em round. (*Crosses and sits top of sofa* L)

(ARAMINTA *comes round* L. *end of table with three cups of tea on tray.*)

GEORGE (*who is sitting apart, shakes his head*). I bain't in trim for revelling
MRS SMERDON. Then you didn't ought to have come. (*Sits on sofa*)

(RICHARD *goes to table and gets two dishes of cakes.* ARAMINTA *takes cups for the three on sofa* L. *As she is coming down* DUNNY-

BRIG *rises, takes a cup from tray and gives it to* LOUISA. *She goes on to sofa to ladies.* RICHARD *follows with cakes, first to sofa.* ARAMINTA *looks round, sees all right, and goes back to her place for tea for* DR. RUNDLE *At the moment of her survey,* RICHARD *is on her* L. *close to sofa. As she goes back,* RICHARD *turns to take cakes to* LOUISA. DUNNYBRIG *intercepts and takes them out of his hand, and takes them to* LOUISA, *and* RICHARD *goes to table and gets a plate of sandwiches* HENRY *places* SOPHIE *in chair on his* R. SUSAN *takes a cup and gives it to* SOPHIE. *He takes a cup for himself* L)

HENRY (*to* SUSAN). Have 'e got a bigger cup, my dear?

(ARAMINTA *offering cups of tea to* MRS SMERDON *and* MRS RUNDLE *on sofa, then goes behind table for fresh tea, etc.*)

SUSAN. No, Mr. Coaker. They be all little things like this
HENRY. This ban't a dolls' tea-party, be it? (*Spreads old handkerchief on his knees.*)

(SUSAN *giggles.*)

When I'm tea drinking, give me a proper *cloam cup* to hold a pint.

(SUSAN *goes back to her place and pours out tea*)

DUNNYBRIG (*having taken plates from* RICHARD *To* LOUISA WINDEATT). Will 'e take a sandwich, or one of these here *pink* things?
LOUISA One of those little ones, thanks (*Takes one.*)
DUNNYBRIG. Don't you starve yourself for the sake of your riding hosses. (*Crosses and puts plate on table and returns with cup of tea which* SUSAN *gives him and sits back of ottoman.*)

(RICHARD *waits a moment, speaking to* ARAMINTA *till* SUSAN *comes back, then goes over to* HENRY *with plate of sandwiches, offering them to him at cue* "*riding hosses.*"

HENRY (*to* RICHARD) Ban't there no red meat, Dick?

(ARAMINTA *gives tea and sugar to* DR. RUNDLE *and sugar to* MRS. SMERDON *and* MRS. RUNDLE, *and goes behind table*)

RICHARD. These here are sandwiches.
HENRY. What little tiddleys! Put 'em there alongside me.

(RICHARD *puts them on chair* L *of* HENRY *and goes to table.* HENRY *places them on his knees and proceeds to gobble them up, and gives* SOPHIE *one. As laugh finishes enter* MISS TAPPER *from garden.*)

MISS TAPPER (R.C.). May I ask those who have finished their tea (*looks at* HENRY) to pass out into the garden?
HENRY. We'm only just starting, my dear.

(RICHARD *turns to* MISS TAPPER *as she goes down.* RICHARD *at table and gets two plates of cakes.*)

RICHARD. Won't you help yourself, miss?

(DUNNYBRIG *and* LOUISA *rise and sit up stage* R. LOUISA *puts her cup on table* R.C.)

MISS TAPPER (R.C.). Not yet—not yet, Mr. Richard. (*Crosses.*) Has Mr. Rundle got some coffee? (L.C.)
MRS. RUNDLE. Yes, thank you.

(MISS TAPPER *comes down between ottoman and sofa,* MRS. RUNDLE *smiles and indicates her cup.* MISS TAPPER *turns and meets* MARY *in front of ottoman* C. *Re-enter* CHURDLES ASH R.)

ASH. Miss Mary Hearn.

(*Enter* MISS MARY HEARN. *Exit* ASH, *closing door.* MARY *is very showily dressed with a grotesque hat full of huge flowers. She is affected and excited and giggles. After her entrance* SUSAN, *admiring* MARY *as she goes over to* HENRY *and collects his cup.*)

MISS TAPPER (C.). How are you, Mary?
MARY (C.). Nicely, thank you. Don't I look it? My!

(MISS TAPPER *steps back to look at* MARY. MARY *turns round and surveys the company.*)

All the world and his wife, I see! How do, Mr. Dunnybrig? How d'ye do, Doctor?

(SUSAN *takes cup from* HENRY *and goes back to behind table.*)

There was a parcel come for you this morning—physic bottles by the look of it. (*Crosses to* HENRY.) How are you, Uncle?
MISS TAPPER (*up* L.C.). Tea for Miss Hearn, please.

(MISS TAPPER *goes up to table. Sees* SUSAN *is busy looking after* HENRY'S *second cup—so she takes* MARY'S *coffee herself from* ARAMINTA.)

MARY. No, coffee—if there's any going. They had iced coffee at the vicarage party, I hear—though I wasn't there myself. (*Crosses to* C. *across* R.)

(DUNNYBRIG *puts his cup on table* R C.)

MISS TAPPER. Here I'm afraid we only have it hot.

(RICHARD *crosses to* DUNNYBRIG *and* LOUISA *with plates of cakes.*)

MARY. Bless you, that's all right—if 'tis hot. (*At this precise moment* MISS TAPPER *hands her the coffee, which is steaming hot.*)

You generally get it lukewarm at a party. (*Sits on ottoman* C.)

(SUSAN *goes to* HENRY *with second cup of tea.*)

HENRY. Coffee wi' ice in it at the vicarage! Good powers! Haven't parson more compassion on the people's bellies? (*Takes cup from* SUSAN.)

(SUSAN *laughs explosively.*)

MISS TAPPER (R.C., *crossing to* SUSAN *behind ottoman*). Susan! Susan!

(SUSAN *crosses in front of* MISS TAPPER *and goes back to table, and* MISS TAPPER *follows her and then crosses back to* LOUISA *and* DUNNYBRIG *up* R C. RICHARD *comes down to* HENRY *with two dishes of cake.* HENRY *endeavours to take both dishes, but* RICHARD *shakes his head and only allows him to take a piece of cake from each dish.* MARY *looks round—sees* GEORGE, *and says,* "Well, Mr. Smerdon." *This holding out her hand, as a challenge to* GEORGE *to come and speak to her. He gets up, rather ashamed at being dragged from his seclusion, and comes down between ottoman and sofa. Shakes hands with her and sits on her* L. RICHARD *comes with cakes on her* R. *During the following scene the different groups must be talking and interested, and take no notice of* MARY, GEORGE, *and* RICHARD.)

(MISS TAPPER *crosses to* LOUISA *and* DUNNYBRIG.)

MARY. Well, Mr. Smerdon, I wish you joy, I'm sure. (*As she shakes hands,* GEORGE *sits* L. *on ottoman.*)

(RICHARD *brings her cakes.* DR. RUNDLE *puts his cup on side table* L.)

Ah, Mr. Richard—being useful for once! (*Taking cake.*) Old Tapper's going it, eh?

RICHARD. Have a cake, George? (*Offering plate across* MARY.)

GEORGE. No—I can't eat.

RICHARD. Well—try to look as if you was alive. (*Goes behind ottoman back to table, puts them down and then comes down* L.C.)

GEORGE. All very fine for you; but you don't know what's happening to me.

MARY (*giggling*). He's in love! (*To* HENRY, *who laughs.*)

GEORGE. Yes, I be in love; and so's this man : and he's cheerful, because, no doubt, 'tis going well with him. But I——

MARY. There's as good fish in the sea than ever came out——

GEORGE. I'll dog her—I'll haunt her—I'll give her no peace. I'll not take "no" for an answer.

(MISS TAPPER *leaves* LOUISA *and* DUNNYBRIG *and crosses to table.*)

MARY. She's said "no," then?

(HENRY *laughs.*)

58   THE FARMER'S WIFE.   [ACT II.

GEORGE. Never you mind what she's said.

(MISS TAPPER *takes* MRS. SMERDON'S *cup.* ARAMINTA *takes it and puts it on table.* RICHARD *laughs heartily* L.C.)

You're too clever, you are.
   MARY. But perhaps 'twas before the legacy. You try again.
   RICHARD (*down* L.C.). And how d'you know I'm in love, George?
   GEORGE. By the way you keep looking at that door.
   MARY. Are you both after the same, I wonder? We shall have some fun if you are. (*Laughs with* HENRY.)

(*Enter* CHURDLES ASH, *announces*)

ASH. My lot! Mr. Samuel Sweetland, Miss Petronell Sweetland, Miss Sibley Sweetland.

(*Enter* PETRONELL *first, then* SIBLEY, *then* SWEETLAND.)

(MISS TAPPER *crosses to* C. *to meet them.*)

MISS TAPPER (C.). Ah, Petronell! (*kiss*)—Sibley (*kiss*).
ASH (*to* SWEETLAND). Just in time! They're hard at it.

(*Exit* R., *closing door.*)

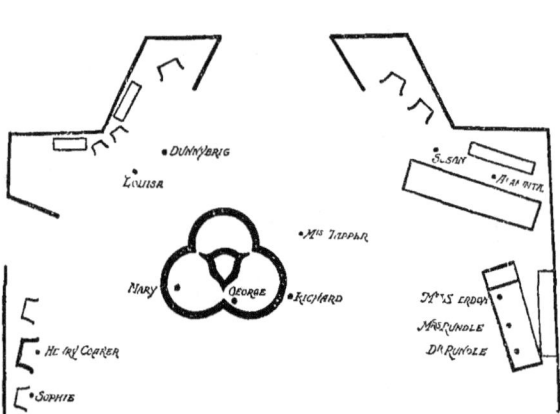

(GEORGE *goes up* L *of settee and meets* PETRONELL. *She does not take much notice of him, as she is looking at* RICHARD. *But she allows herself to be taken by* GEORGE *to chair up* L. *of window, where she sits.* RICHARD *meets* SIBLEY *just above, and a little* R *of ottoman.* SWEETLAND *is the last to be received by* MISS TAPPER. *He waits for her* R.C. *above and between door and ottoman. He hardly takes the hand she offers*)

MISS TAPPER. So good of you all to come!

Act II.] THE FARMER'S WIFE. 59

(MARY *rises and beckons* DR. RUNDLE. PETRONELL *and* SIBLEY *have passed on to* GEORGE *and* RICHARD.)

SWEETLAND (*to* MISS TAPPER). You can kiss *them*, I see!

(*After his line to her, he comes down to* HENRY *and speaks to him. He puts* SOPHIE *under the chin. When* SOPHIE *crosses to* L. SWEETLAND *sits in her chair, which is* R. *of armchair, and talks to* HENRY.)

(MISS TAPPER *crosses* R. *end of table.* LOUISA *rises and crosses down towards sofa—pausing to speak to* SIBLEY, DR. RUNDLE, *and nodding to* MRS. SMERDON *and* MRS. RUNDLE, *and sits in seat vacated by* DR. RUNDLE. PETRONELL *sits when* GEORGE *puts her in chair up* L. *by window.* DR. RUNDLE *and* MARY *meet* C.)

MARY. Look at those ridiculous girls!

(RICHARD *goes to table for plate of cakes.*)

Which is going to be Mrs. George Smerdon, I wonder?
DR. RUNDLE. He won't have to ask a girl twice.
MARY. Her pill will be coated with gold, anyway.

(MARY *goes up* L. *of ottoman up to window, pausing to speak to* SIBLEY. DR. RUNDLE *goes up* R. *of ottoman, meeting* LOUISA *and pausing to speak to* SIBLEY, *and joins* MARY *in window.*)

GEORGE (R. *of* PETRONELL. *Now grown lively, to* PETRONELL). Will you have tea or coffee? There's both here.
PETRONELL. Thanks—anything.

(DUNNYBRIG *goes down to* HENRY *and after putting cup and saucer and plate on table sits above him.* RICHARD *goes to below ottoman, crossing below* DR. RUNDLE *and* LOUISA *with plate, and beckons* SIBLEY.)

GEORGE Well, don't you move from this spot till I come back I'll sweep the table for you. (*He goes to table and collects all that he can carry.*)

(SOPHIE *crosses* L. *to* LOUISA. SWEETLAND *sits chair below* HENRY. GEORGE *has taken* PETRONELL *up* L. *and puts her into chair* L. *of window, meaning to keep her there all to himself.* SIBLEY *near table* R C.)

SIBLEY. Here's a seat, Petronell. Richard's beckoning.

(PETRONELL *comes down behind* GEORGE *to* L. *front of ottoman and sits on it* SIBLEY *sits on her* R. GEORGE *with his back to room, busy collecting at table, does not see her, and turns up* L *to find her gone.* RICHARD *has gone up to lower end of table and fetched cakes, and* ARAMINTA *brings two cups of tea on tray to* SIBLEY. GEORGE, *laden, turns, sees* PETRONELL, *finds he is too late, and with a savage look at* RICHARD *he puts things back on table. Then he goes to top corner of table. They go to the seats and* ARAMINTA *brings them tea.* MISS TAPPER *takes* MRS. RUNDLE'S *cup and puts it on table.* SUSAN *takes a dish of cakes to* HENRY. SOPHIE *crosses to* LOUISA *with her cup and saucer and sits on her knee, takes off her hat and gives it to* MRS. SMERDON.)

SIBLEY (*rising*). You're tired to death, 'Minta; do let me help you. (*Takes cup of tea from* ARAMINTA.)

(ARAMINTA *crossing round ottoman on* R. *of* SIBLEY *in front of* PETRONELL)

ARAMINTA. Not a bit. 'Tis a splendid party and all going like a marriage bell. (*Tea to* PETRONELL *and back behind table*)

(SIBLEY *sits again* R. *of ottoman. After putting plates down* GEORGE *returns to find* PETRONELL *has moved and goes and stands by end of table.* MISS TAPPER *arranging table for* SWEETLAND *to sit.*)

HENRY (*to* SUSAN). Not another bit, my dear. I be blowed out like a balloon a'ready.

(SUSAN *giggles, nearly dropping cakes, then offers to* SWEETLAND, *who refuses.* RICHARD *puts plates on table.*)

'Tis fantastic food. But what don't fatten, fills. Where's my stick?

(SWEETLAND *picks it up and gives it to him.*)

Be us to have a bit of fun in the garden?

(RICHARD *sits back of ottoman.*)

SUSAN. Yes, Mr. Coaker. There's four men come all the way from Plymouth. (*Goes back to table and replaces cakes and goes behind table.*)

(MARY *comes in from window and sits* R. DR. RUNDLE *goes to* GEORGE, *they talk for a moment.* MISS TAPPER, *who, after speaking to* SWEETLAND, *has gone over to table.* SWEETLAND *finds himself facing* ARAMINTA, *who, with a pleasant smile, offers him a cup of coffee. They talk together.* DUNNYBRIG *has come down to* HENRY *and is now sitting in chair on his* L. GEORGE *goes into window.*)

HENRY (*to* MR. DUNNYBRIG). Be there any spirits or cordials to top up with and steady the victuals, Valiant?

(SWEETLAND *rises, crosses up and meets* DR. RUNDLE *and shakes hands and goes to table* C.)

DUNNYBRIG (*seated*). No, Henry. There's nothing like that. These old maiden ladies be like kittens. They don't think there's any better drink than milk.

MISS TAPPER (*coming from table below* SWEETLAND *to* R.C. *above* SIBLEY). May we have your song now, Sibley dear—before we go into the garden?

ACT II.] THE FARMER'S WIFE. 61

RICHARD (C., *rises*). Hush! Hush! Miss Sweetland's going to sing.

(GEORGE *in window* C. *The company generally are chattering and laughing, and have not taken much notice of* RICHARD. DUNNYBRIG *rises to enforce silence and sits again.*)

DUNNYBRIG (*rises*). Hush, all, for Samuel Sweetland's daughter! (*Sits again.*)
LOUISA (*on sofa* L., *down stage end*). She's got a voice like a robin —so sweet and so happy.
HENRY. God send 'tis a funny song! Us can do with a good laugh after a good guzzle.
SIBLEY (*on ottoman*). I'll do my best, but I'm very simple at it.
PETRONELL (*on ottoman*). Sing "Blue Eyes," Sibley.
SIBLEY. All right. (*Rises and goes up with* MISS TAPPER L. *Puts cup on small table up* R.C.)

(RICHARD *is standing, more or less back to audience, and addresses the company generally.*)

RICHARD (*with his mouth full*). Miss Sweetland's song be called "Blue Eyes."

(GEORGE *comes down from window to* L *of* PETRONELL.)

GEORGE (*to* PETRONELL). Why for ain't 'e going to sing?
PETRONELL. Miss Tapper didn't ask me.
GEORGE. More fool her! (*Stands* L.C. *by ottoman, biting his nails and gazing at* PETRONELL.)

(*Re-enter* CHURDLES ASH.)

ASH (*announcing*). The Reverend Tudor.

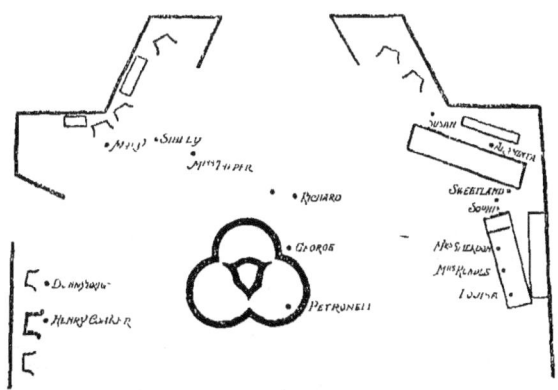

(*Enter the* VICAR, *the* REV. SEPTIMUS TUDOR.)

Miss Tapper (R C.). Ah, Vicar! (*They shake hands.*) Better late than never I do hope your dear mother is going to honour me?

Vicar (R.C.) Her Bath chair has been wheeled into the garden.

Ash (*by door*). The Honourable Mrs. Tudor be in the veranda.

(*Exit, closing door.*)

(*The Bath chair is wheeled on from* R. *When in position it is outside the window* L. *end, facing down* L. *The* Nurse *stands behind.* Miss Tapper *goes to* Mrs Tudor *to welcome her as she is in place* Dr. Rundle *goes to her immediately after and talks to her, also* Mrs. Rundle, *and* Mrs. Smerdon *takes* Mrs Rundle's *place.*)

Vicar (*smiles round at the company generally and comes down a bit* R.C.). Ah, Mr. Croaker!

(Sophie *takes her cup and saucer to table and sits on top arm of sofa.* Sweetland *sits on edge of table.*)

Henry. Farmer Sweetland's maid be just going to sing a song, your reverence.

(Miss Tapper *comes down* R C. *and* Mrs Rundle *goes and sits in chair* R. *by window* Araminta *and* Susan *sit on form behind table. The* Vicar *then turns to* Henry, *nods to* Dunnybrig *and sits in chair* R. *of* Henry, *when* Miss Tapper *says,* "Will you be seated, Vicar?")

Vicar Don't let me interrupt.
Miss Tapper (R.C., R. *of* Vicar) Will you be seated, Vicar?
Henry. Sit here alongside me. (*Tapping chair with stick.*)

(Richard *sits* R. *on ottoman, facing* Sibley. *The* Vicar *sits.*)

Miss Tapper. Now, Sibley dear!

(Dr Rundle *sees that* Mrs Tudor *is in good position for song and, if necessary, slightly adjusts chair. She is almost in the room.* Sweetland *leans back against table, watching* Sibley *with fatherly pride* Araminta *and* Susan *sitting on form behind table.* George *stands* L *of* Petronell. Richard *sits on ottoman facing* Sibley. Miss Tapper *has fussed generally to get everybody in place, and sits ottoman, at back of it. The movements immediately before and after the song are almost simultaneous in each case They only take a few seconds, and after the song do not interrupt dialogue which follows on as soon as applause subsides.*)

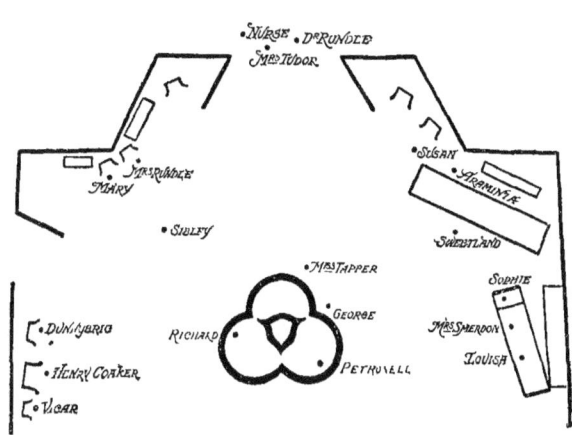

(SIBLEY *stands in the midst and sings sweetly and simply without any self-consciousness.*)

SIBLEY (*sings*). Oh, Daisy dear, wi' eyes so blue,
Come, tell me quick, and tell me true,
If I be your man, or the chap in grey—
Him as drove 'e to market but yesterday!
Ah! (*Hums.*) Him as drove 'e to market but yesterday!

Why, Billy Blue, now don't 'e frown,
And don't 'e look up, nor don't 'e look down,
But look straight into my eyes so blue—
For 'tis there you can see whether I love you.
Ah! (*Hums.*) For 'tis there you can see whether I love you.

Now Billy stared with all his might,
And fondly thought that he'd seen aright.
But up'long to worship the next Sunday
If her wasn't axed out with the chap in grey:
Ah! (*Hums.*) Yes, he'd put up the banns, thicky chap in grey.

HENRY. Good—good! Ha-ha!—a proper song! (*Banging floor with stick.*)

(RICHARD *signs to his uncle.*)

SIBLEY. There's one more verse, Mr. Coaker.

(*The* VICAR *taps* HENRY *on the arm, and* HENRY *glares at him. The* VICAR *crosses his legs.* MISS TAPPER *rises*)

MISS TAPPER. Hush! Hush! (*Re-seats herself.*)

SIBLEY (*sings*). Now Billy's swearing, so 'tis said,
That a man be a fool to trust a maid,
And the devil, tho' black as a parson's shoe,
Have doubtless got eyes of a beautiful blue—
Ah! (*Hums.*) Billy knows that his eyes be a beautiful blue.

(*After the song there is applause from all, particularly* RICHARD, *and* SWEETLAND *beams with pride and rises. Then there is a general move.* MISS TAPPER *goes to* SIBLEY, *thanks her and goes to* R. *of* MRS. TUDOR. DR. RUNDLE *joins* SIBLEY R C. SOPHIE *gets up and goes to* ARAMINTA *at table.* PETRONELL *moves to sofa, shakes hands with* LOUISA *and* MRS SMERDON *and sits top end of sofa.* MARY *moves down to* RICHARD'S *place on ottoman.* MARY *tries to talk to* GEORGE, *but he only has eyes for* PETRONELL. RICHARD *goes up to* R.C *of window and talks to* DR. RUNDLE, *and* SIBLEY, *handing her her teacup from small table.* DUNNYBRIG *gets up and stands* R. *of ottoman just above and facing the* VICAR *and* HENRY. MRS. RUNDLE *rises and goes and stands* L. *of* MRS. TUDOR *on the veranda.*)

DUNNYBRIG (*rises*, R.C.). Be the devil so black as your shoe, Vicar?

VICAR (*seated*). Miss Sweetland should choose something more refined. She sings quite prettily. You haven't forgotten our harvest festival, Mr. Dunnybrig, or you, Mr. Coaker?

DUNNYBRIG. The Lord of the Harvest have smote the harvest this year. It ain't a time for making any fuss about it, in my opinion. Least said soonest mended. (*Goes over in front of ottoman to* LOUISA *and stands* L.C. *back to audience.*)

HENRY (*seated*). Yes, we must forgive and forget, and hope next year the Almighty will do to others same as He'd be done by.

(SIBLEY, RICHARD *and* DR. RUNDLE *up* R C.)

VICAR (*seated*). A harvest festival embraces all the fruits of the earth.

HENRY. So it do, no doubt. I've got some vegetable marrows fat as little pigs. You can have 'em for the church windows, and us be drawing turnips a'ready—proper masterpieces—so round and white

(*Bus.* MARY *and* HENRY, *who takes out his pipe and tobacco-box*)

VICAR. Really! How remarkable! (*Gets up and goes up* R C, *turns and looks reproachfully at* HENRY. *Then turns in direction of* DR RUNDLE *and* RICHARD *and* SIBLEY *and they talk.*)

(MISS TAPPER *comes down* C. *as* VICAR *goes up.* HENRY *bus. pipe and tobacco.*)

MISS TAPPER (*down* C.) Shall we pass into the garden now? (*Goes to* MRS. TUDOR.)

DUNNYBRIG (*to* LOUISA WINDEATT, *helping her up*). Come along. 'Tis getting a bit fuggy in here.

LOUISA. Are you coming, Petronell?

(DUNNYBRIG *goes to table, stands there with* LOUISA. PETRONELL *goes up to* RICHARD *and* SIBLEY, *and the two girls go off into the garden together with their teacups.* MRS. SMERDON *takes* SOPHIE *off* C. *to* L. GEORGE, *after a look off after* PETRONELL, *goes and joins* DR. RUNDLE, *to* R. MISS TAPPER *looks round and goes out into veranda to talk to* MRS. TUDOR.)

MRS. SMERDON. Come, Sophie—Sophie, don't you eat no more. Here's Miss Dench dog-tired, I'm sure, and glad to see the last of us.

(MRS. SMERDON *goes to* SOPHIE *and takes her up to window.* MRS. TUDOR *speaks to* SOPHIE. SIBLEY *turns and meets* RICHARD R. *of window and speaks to him.*)

(SUSAN *crosses and exits door* R.)

(ARAMINTA *comes to* L. *end of table, talks to* LOUISA—*with cup of tea ready for* VICAR.)

(*As* DUNNYBRIG *and* LOUISA *go up* SWEETLAND *comes down* L. *from table to* L. *side of ottoman.*)

SWEETLAND (*to* MARY). Shall I get you anything more to eat or drink?

MARY. I'll have one of they red plums, I think.

(*The* VICAR *comes* L. *of and above* MARY. SWEETLAND *goes to table for dish.* RICHARD *goes and sits below* HENRY R.)

(*Now off:* SIBLEY, PETRONELL, MRS. SMERDON, SOPHIE. *Exit* SUSAN MAINE R.)

VICAR (*coming to them*). Ah, Miss Hearn—escaped from your duties for a little while!

MARY. Yes, your reverence.

VICAR (*to* SWEETLAND, *who is now beside the table with his dish of plums*). Ah, neighbour! I hope I see you well.

(MISS TAPPER *talking to* MRS. TUDOR *up* C.)

SWEETLAND (*holding up dish of plums proudly to* VICAR *on his* R.). I gave her those—finest things on the table

VICAR (*picks up a plum and then replaces it*) They remind me of our approaching harvest festival. You won't forget the church?

(DR. RUNDLE *and* GEORGE *sit up* R. *by door.*)

SWEETLAND. Drat the festivals! (*Crosses in front of* VICAR *to* MARY, *who takes a plum.*)

E

(*She takes a bite but never really eats it; she carries it off with her.*)

They come round quicker than quarter day. I ain't got no corn this year—nobody has.

(*He takes dish back to table and returns and sits* L. *of* MARY, *after* LOUISA *has gone up. When* SWEETLAND *is seated the* VICAR *looks round, goes to table and speaks a word to* LOUISA)

(MISS TAPPER *comes in during this by window and goes* R. *and back of ottoman and then to table above the* VICAR)

VICAR. I hope Mrs. Windeatt will be kinder.

(ARAMINTA *gives him a cup of tea. He takes a small piece of cake*)

(*Exit* LOUISA *and* DUNNYBRIG *speaking to* MRS. TUDOR *as they pass* C. *to* L.)

(*Enter* R. SUSAN *with tray of ices and stands* R.C, *and* ASH, *who remains by door, closing it, and talking to* DR. RUNDLE)

MISS TAPPER. Ices are coming into the garden for those that like them. Ask Mrs. Tudor first, Susan. Miss Dench—Miss Dench, would you please carry them?

(SWEETLAND *sits on* L. *of ottoman.* ARAMINTA *crosses, takes tray of ices and goes out* C., *followed by* SUSAN. MRS. TUDOR *and* MRS. RUNDLE *take ices, and* ARAMINTA *and* SUSAN *go off* L.)

Why, Vicar, you have nothing to eat!
VICAR. On the contrary, I'm doing remarkably well—making a splendid tea. (*Shows half a small piece of cake.*)

(MISS TAPPER *takes a plate of cakes up to* MRS. TUDOR, *who takes one.*)

HENRY (*beckons to* RICHARD). Help me up, Dick, will 'e?

(RICHARD *rises and takes his right arm to keep him up and they go up* R.C.)

Can us smoke in the flower-garden, Churdles Ash?

(MISS TAPPER *with* MRS TUDOR.)

ASH (*by door*). What be a flower-garden for, Henry?

(*The* VICAR *puts cup and saucer on table.*)

HENRY. Right! I'll chance it.

(*The* VICAR *crosses and gives* HENRY *his left arm.* RICHARD *on* HENRY'S R. VICAR *on his* L)

VICAR. Let me give you an arm, Mr. Coaker.

(MISS TAPPER *comes down and replaces plate on table.*)

HENRY. Thank you kindly, your reverence. I'd do the same for you. This here fancy food makes me feel so light as a cloud. (*Hiccup*)

RICHARD. I'll look after uncle, your reverence.

(*The* VICAR *joins* GEORGE *and* DR. RUNDLE, *who rise. Exeunt* HENRY *and* RICHARD C. *to* L)

(*As soon as they have gone* MISS TAPPER *nods to* ASH *and indicates* MRS. TUDOR.)

ASH (R.C). The old lady—I'll shove her to Monkey Puzzle. (ASH *takes handle of Bath chair and wheels off* C. *and* L. *and go under steps*.)

(MRS. TUDOR *out of sight off* L. MRS. RUNDLE *walking off in front of them*.)

(*Now off:* ARAMINTA, SUSAN, RICHARD, HENRY, MRS. TUDOR, MRS. RUNDLE, ASH, MRS. SMERDON, SOPHIE, DUNNYBRIG, *and* LOUISA. SIBLEY *and* PETRONELL)

MISS TAPPER (*coming down* L.C. *to* SWEETLAND). You'll come into the garden and hear the Glee Singers, won't you?

SWEETLAND. Don't you trouble your head about me—I'm talking to Miss Hearn

(MISS TAPPER *goes away into garden* C. *to* L.)

MARY. Let's get outside.

SWEETLAND. Have another plum?

MARY (*rises and crosses front and up* L.C.). No, no!—enough's as good as a feast.

(SWEETLAND *rises.* MARY *stops up* L C.)

And don't you follow me about so close—you'll have the people talking. You know what the village is.

(*Exeunt* MARY *and* SWEETLAND C. *to* R.)

VICAR (*up* R.C. *to* GEORGE—*they come down a bit*). I have heard of your good fortune. It is a solemn responsibility, and I hope you won't forget the Giver.

GEORGE. No; I be going to put up a white marble stone to him, when his grave have settled down. I dare say I'll spend twenty pound or more. And did I ought to share the money with my brother Tom, Vicar?

VICAR. That is a serious question I cannot answer in a moment, George.

GEORGE I ain't getting no fun out of it yet, anyway.

(SUSAN *and* SIBLEY *and* ARAMINTA *come back from the garden.*

ARAMINTA *and* SUSAN *tidy up behind table.* SIBLEY *helps.* SUSAN *at end of table starts to eat.*)

VICAR. The money that gives us most pleasure to spend is that which we devote to others. You will not forget your own parish—I feel sure of that.

(MISS TAPPER *enters* C.)

MISS TAPPER (*at the window*). The Glee Singers are about to begin. Will you come into the garden, Vicar, and you, Doctor, and you, Mr. Smerdon ?

(*The* VICAR *and* MISS TAPPER *go out.*)

DR. RUNDLE. Now's the time, George !

(DR. RUNDLE *helping himself from the table up* L.)

GEORGE. I ain't hungry to-day.

(*Exit* GEORGE C. *to* R.)

DR. RUNDLE. Come along, Miss Sibley.

(ARAMINTA *puts vase of flowers from* C. *to* R. *of table.*)

SIBLEY. I'm looking after Araminta. I'll come along presently.

(*Exit* DR. RUNDLE C. *to* L.)

For goodness' sake sit down and rest, 'Minta ! You'll drop if you don't Sit here and take it easy.

(*Enter* CHURDLES ASH.)

ASH. Give me something to drink. (*Comes down to* C. *of big table, bringing chair from up* L. *Sits, takes off his gloves and wipes his bald head with them*) Thank the Lord I ain't a indoor man. I be gasping for air and tobacco.

(SUSAN *gives him lemonade and cakes with cream.*)

SUSAN (*by table*). Take one o' these, Mr. Ash.
ASH. Anything—everything ! 'Tis my turn now. (*Eating.*) Here, stuff one of these down your neck, 'Minta. There's cream in 'em.

(ARAMINTA *sits behind table with* SIBLEY)

ARAMINTA. I'm sure it have all gone off most glorious—not a hitch, and everybody as happy as kings and queens.
SIBLEY. Except father. There's something the matter with him
ARAMINTA. And your lovely song—'twas the crown of the party.

(*Enter* MISS TAPPER *hurriedly* C. *from* L.)

Miss Tapper. Fruit—fruit in the garden, please!

(*Warn Singers.*)

(*Exit* Miss Tapper c. *to* l. *All look after her.*)

Ash. Dark old dragon! She'd run the soles off your feet. (*Turn to table.*)

Susan (*by table*). Let her wait A proper tyrant she is

Araminta. No, no! (*Rises.*) Now's the moment for fruit. (*Gives* Susan *dish of plums*)

Sibley. Finish your tea first, 'Minta. (*Goes up to* c)

(Ash *picks up dish of cakes.*)

(Susan *goes off* c. *to* l. *with dish of plums*)

Araminta. I've done. (*Goes to side table and takes glass dish of fruit.*)

(*Enter* Petronell c. *from* l.)

Petronell. Where's father?

(*Exit* Ash *with plate of cakes.*)

(Petronell *comes down* r.)

Sibley. He went into the garden with Miss Hearn.

(Araminta *coming in front of table. Exit* Sibley c. *to* l.)

Petronell. I'm sick of this, 'Minta. I never was at such a stupid party.

Araminta. Don't say that. Where's Richard? He'll cheer you up.

Petronell. 'Tis for him to find me, I should think—not for me to find him.

(*Enter* George Smerdon *from* r. *They—*Araminta *and* George—*pass each other.*)

(*Exit* Araminta c. *to* l. *with dish of fruit.*)

(George *speaks, coming down.*)

George. Petronell, you might give me a minute. I only came to the party to see you.

Petronell (*sits in despair in armchair down* r.). Don't start again on me, there's a good man.

George (r.c. *by ottoman*). I haven't begun yet. You don't know what you're in for. There's no escape for you. It have got to be said over and over again till you grasp hold of it.

(*Glee begins—*" Sleep, gentle lady.")

Petronell. I have grasped hold of it.

GEORGE. No, you haven't You haven't had time. But you will, I'm so solid and steadfast as a rock. (*Sits on* R *front of ottoman facing her.*) I can't change, Petronell.

PETRONELL. I can't change either.

GEORGE. It may surprise you to know that it grows worse, instead of better, with me.

PETRONELL. I said "no" as clear as a girl could speak it.

GEORGE. I ban't built to hear "no." I won't hear "no"! I'm going to be at you as steady as Time, till you say "yes." 'Twill wear you to a shadow I shouldn't wonder. But there's no escape.

PETRONELL. It's not reasonable, George.

GEORGE. I don't know nothing about reason. A man like me is far above reason. I'm never beat. I go on my way like the wind and the wave—never tired. I shall keep offering you—off and on—till I'm grey-headed, and you've got a foot in the grave.

(PETRONELL *rises and goes up* R. *level with door.*)

I only tell you this, Petronell, because you may think I'm like certain other weak chaps that you've choked off at a word.

PETRONELL (*facing him*) Then I see there's but one thing will stop you, George.

GEORGE. There isn't one thing—only death.

PETRONELL. There's got to be one.

(*She is much tried, but contrives to keep her temper.*)

I love another man—there!

GEORGE (*rises*). What's his name?

PETRONELL. You mustn't ask that.

GEORGE. Why not?

PETRONELL. Oh, you're so difficult, George. You've got no proper feeling where a woman's concerned. (*Walks up to window*)

GEORGE (*rises, comes round by* L. *of ottoman and joins her on her* L.) What's his name? That's what I want to know; and I will know

PETRONELL. I can't tell you.

(*They come back to original position level with door*)

GEORGE. Do he love you? Have he made the fine love to you what I have? Would he do all for you I would?

PETRONELL. I wonder what you would do, if it came to the point?

GEORGE. I'd do all a strong man with five thousand pounds behind him could do.

PETRONELL (*sits again in armchair down* R.). It isn't money, George.

GEORGE (*sits on chair above armchair, moving it a little nearer to hers and a little to her* L). You hate farming, so I'd throw it all up and start a shop, because I know you like shops.

PETRONELL. Would you do that?

GEORGE Would t'other chap? Why, I'd get any sort of shop in the world You should choose what you liked, from fish and poultry to gold watches.

PETRONELL (*thinking for a moment and looking in front of her. This encourages him a little and he becomes more ardent*). I'd love a shop! A tobacconist's shop.

GEORGE. Then love me and we'll start a shop (*Takes her hand.*)

PETRONELL (*draws her hand away*). You can't make yourself love a man.

GEORGE. Why not? If I can love you like a burning fiery furnace, why the hell can't you love me the same?

PETRONELL. Don't I tell you I love somebody else? (*Rises and crosses up* R C)

GEORGE. Well, keep the shop in your mind. Don't lose sight of the shop.

(PETRONELL *starts and looks towards the window as* SIBLEY *enters, followed by* RICHARD C *from* L.)

(*Exit* PETRONELL C. *to* R.)

(GEORGE *rises and goes to door* R) I'm sick of this. I ain't enjoying myself. I'm going back home now. Where's mother and Sophie?

RICHARD Not enjoying yourself, George?

GEORGE. I don't want no words with you, Richard Coaker 'Tis war to the knife between us, and now you know it.

(SIBLEY *sits* C)

(*Second glee begins*—" The Pump.")

(*Exit* GEORGE SMERDON *door* R., *closing it*)

RICHARD (*comes down* L. *of* SIBLEY). Well—what d'you think of that? What have I done to vex George?

SIBLEY. He's troubled seemingly.

RICHARD But why with me? (*Coming down* L.C.) His money be going to ruin that man.

SIBLEY. Poor George!

RICHARD. I ain't sorry for him. (L C. *by sofa*.) But I'm terrible sorry for myself.

SIBLEY. Why, Dick?

RICHARD. Because I'm such an everyday, stupid sort of chap— no money, and never done nothing to name

SIBLEY. Every lover's done the finest thing in the whole world in the eyes of the girl who loves him.

RICHARD. And what's that?

SIBLEY. Why, fall in love with her. That's the mightiest thing of all—if she feels the same.

RICHARD. And waste of time if she don't. No doubt George Smerdon would chuck up all his money if Petronell loved him.

SIBLEY. Her heart's gone.

RICHARD. Solemn truth? (*Pause. He sits on sofa* L.) That's terrible interesting. And does she know what the man's feeling?

SIBLEY. I reckon so. But he hangs fire a bit.

RICHARD (*away from her*). If you be in love, you get terrible quick to mark the signs in another person, no doubt. (*Turns to her.*) If Petronell can see a man loves her, then—my girl might see the same—eh?

SIBLEY. Naturally.

RICHARD. And wouldn't think none the worse of me?

SIBLEY. Of course not.

RICHARD (*gets up and is going to sit by her*). Why—then——

(*Glee Singers a little louder.*)

(*Enter* SAMUEL SWEETLAND *and* MARY HEARN.)

(PETRONELL *appears at window from* R.)

(SWEETLAND *comes* C. *to back of settee.* MARY *remains for a moment up* L.C. *by table drinking lemonade and selecting a cake.*)

SWEETLAND. Tell 'em to harness up, Dick Coaker, please.

(SIBLEY *rises and joins* PETRONELL.)

RICHARD. Oh! (*Goes in front of settee to door* R.)

SWEETLAND. I've promised to give Miss Hearn a lift home.

(*Exit* RICHARD *door* R., *closing it.*)

(*Exit* PETRONELL C. *to* L., *with* SIBLEY.)

MARY (*taking a glass of lemonade*). 'Tis a silly, fussy affair—just what you'd expect from a silly, fussy old maid. (*Drinks.*)

SWEETLAND Never mind her I came here a purpose to see you, so just wait a minute. I'll shut the windows. (*Shuts windows. Glee Singers cease.*) You can't hear yourself speak, such a yowling going on.

MARY (*takes up plate and chooses a cake*). What did she want music for? Every woman would sooner hear herself talk than another person sing.

SWEETLAND. Of course she would—if she'd got a voice like yours.

(*Bus. They laugh together.*)

MARY (*goes down* L., *sits on ottoman eating her cake*). D'you believe in fortune-telling, Mr. Sweetland? I had mine told by a gipsy, and she said I was going to be a wife inside a year.

SWEETLAND. Well done, her! I'm sure I hope that's true. (*Sits on her* R.)

MARY. I've been in a twitter about it ever since. A fine handsome chap with high shoulders and blue eyes, and very well to do, and——

SWEETLAND. That sounds mighty like somebody I know, Mary.

MARY. Of course you do. So do we all.

SWEETLAND. If I looked in the looking-glass I should see him—eh? (*Nudges* MARY.)

MARY (*giggles*). You—you! You—at your age! Well, I never! (*Laughs*.)

SWEETLAND. You don't want to marry a boy, do you?

MARY (*much annoyed*). Well, and why not? 'Tis a way with boys to marry girls, ain't it?

SWEETLAND. *Girls!* Have you got the face to call yourself a girl?

MARY (*getting excited*). And what the mischief should I call myself? What do you call me?

SWEETLAND. Full blown and a bit over——

MARY. Oh!! (*Takes out handkerchief.*)

SWEETLAND. —that's what I call you. And if you wasn't a back number like myself—like myself, Mary Hearn—I shouldn't be sitting alongside you now.

MARY. Me—me a back number! And you call yourself a gentleman, I suppose! Perhaps you'll be surprised to hear, Mr. Samuel Sweetland, that next birthday I'm——

SWEETLAND. Hush! Don't touch figures. Don't palter with the truth. I know.

MARY. Oh—but——

SWEETLAND. 'Tis in the church register.

MARY. Oh—— (*Throws cake away.*)

SWEETLAND. I looked up your date there not an hour ago. You was born in——

MARY. Coward! (*Gets up.*) A beastly, poking, prying jackdaw, that's what you are! (*Goes to chair by table.*)

SWEETLAND. And what are you? Who opens the letters at the post office?

MARY. OH!!!

SWEETLAND. I never believed it till now; but now I do. And if you can call me " a poking, prying jackdaw," Mary Hearn, I'm wasting your time and mine. You've done it now! It's all over—you've lost the chance of a lifetime, you stupid woman!

MARY. 'Tis libel to say I touch the letters (*goes to him* C.) and I'll have you up for it.

SWEETLAND. No, you won't—you wouldn't dare. There's too many think the same.

MARY. Oh!!

SWEETLAND I can look at you now without a throb or a pang. Here was I—a man out of the common by all accounts—and you—a good enough woman, though too fond of dressing your mutton lamb fashion

MARY. Oh!!! You dare say that! (*To ottoman*)

SWEETLAND. I was going to dare all things. I was just going to say something as you've never heard afore, Mary Hearn, and never will again.

MARY (*staring at him*). I don't know what you're talking about. (*Sits on sofa.*)

SWEETLAND. Oh, yes, you do—nobody better. Trust a woman for that. I came expecting to find good value. I came as a Christian widow man to a Christian spinster.

MARY (*gets up, stares at him*). Is this a nightmare?

SWEETLAND. Your hat is.

(MARY HEARN *sits again sofa* L.)

You've lost the chance of a lifetime—that's what you've done. You're the sort that be so busy running after the boys, that you miss the men—that's what you are. And me one of they people a little child can lead, though a regiment of soldiers can't drive.

MARY. Now, look here. Are you offering marriage, or ain't you?

SWEETLAND. Not now. (*Rises.*) It's all off now—and so will I be. You don't want to hear a " beastly, poking, prying, jackdaw " no more, of course. (*Going up to door.*)

(MARY HEARN *begins to heave and make strange noises*)

(*Turns and comes down a bit.*) I don't care a damn for they noises. You can roll your eyes and gasp and gurgle, or stand on your silly head if you want to. There's the truth, and now you know it.

MARY (*laughing and losing her self-control, gets up and crosses to ottoman*). You—you—you old sheep! You come to a woman in all her prime and beauty—you to run after me!

SWEETLAND (R.C.). And don't you think you was the first, because you wasn't!

MARY (*by ottoman. Pointing at him*). There—there—you've given yourself away properly now! No, I wasn't the first—and I shan't be the last. *I shan't be the last,* Sammy Sweetland! You mind that! (*Sits on ottoman*)

SWEETLAND. Bah! Grapes are sour! You're mad to think what you've lost, you idiot!

MARY (*flinging herself about on ottoman and going into hysterics*). Help! Help! Save me! (*Shrieks wildly.*)

(SWEETLAND *walks down* R *and up and then down again.*)

(*Glee Singers*—" Widdicombe Fair.")

Act II.]   THE FARMER'S WIFE.   75

(*The French windows open and* Miss Tapper *enters, followed by* Henry Coaker *from* L.)

Henry. Guy Fawkes and angels! What's Sammy Sweetland doing to post-mistress?

(Sweetland *standing* R., Mary *on ottoman making horrible noises, kicking, and exposing a considerable length of leg.* Miss Tapper *down on her* L. Henry R. *of and just above ottoman.*)

Mary. Take him away! Take the beast away!

(*Enter from* R. Valiant Dunnybrig *and* Louisa Windeatt, *and go* L.)

Miss Tapper. Where's Dr. Rundle? Quick! Quick!

(*Outside the Glee Singers are singing* "Widdicombe Fair.")

(*Enter* Richard Coaker, Petronell, *and* Sibley. Richard *goes to* L. *by ottoman.*)

The doctor! The doctor!

(Richard *runs back to garden.*)

(Sibley *and* Petronell *go to* Sweetland R.)

(*Enter from* L. Mrs. Smerdon, Dr. Rundle, Vicar, Churdles Ash, *and four Glee Singers. Enter* R. Araminta—Sophie, Teddy, *and* Mrs. Rundle.)

Sweetland. God's my judge I was only talking sense to the fool

Henry. But what was you *doing*, Samuel?

CURTAIN

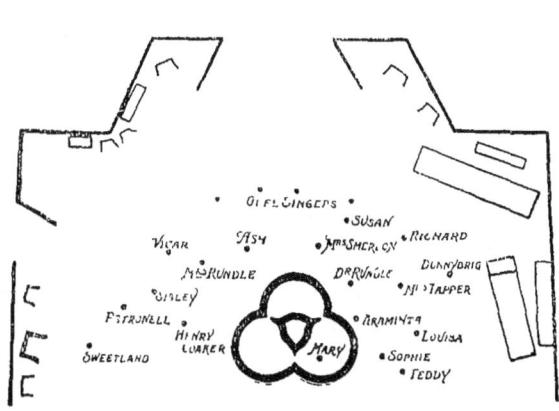

ACT III

SCENE.—*The scene is the same as in Act I, with slight modifications of detail.*

(ARAMINTA DENCH *and* SIBLEY *discovered.* SIBLEY, *behind* L. *of table, is rolling paste and making an apple-pie.* ARAMINTA, *in same place as in Act I, near door to garden, sits peeling potatoes and dropping them into a saucepan of water. The peel she drops into a pail.*)

SIBLEY. I suppose Churdles knows when the train comes in?
ARAMINTA. He knows.
SIBLEY. Father writes as though he wasn't any the better for his little change. And Petronell won't be in a very good temper either.
ARAMINTA. She only went to Dawlish to see if Dick Coaker would be drawn down after her.
SIBLEY. I can't understand why he wasn't. 'Twas a great chance for him.
ARAMINTA. We're all wrong about Richard, Sibley—all wrong. I'm terrible sorry for Petronell.
SIBLEY. It makes me angry with Richard—almost. I told him as plain as I dared at Miss Tapper's spread that he'd only got to ask . . . (*Crying a little.*) There—talk of something else.

(*Enter* CHURDLES ASH R., *closes door.*)

ASH. No news of master?
SIBLEY. We haven't heard this morning.
ASH. Then he's drawn blank again. (*Hangs up hat and goes up* R C.)
SIBLEY. Whatever do you mean, Churdles?
ASH (*going up* R C.). I mean the Dawlish widow at "The Ring o' Bells." Be everybody blind but me?

(ASH *is between* ARAMINTA *and* SIBLEY *in front of doorway*)

Did he go to Dawlish to hear the niggers on the beach? No—he went for a wife and haven't got her. And he'll come back in a proper tantrum, mark me.
ARAMINTA. What be the women made of nowadays?
ASH. Same old beastly stuff they always was. (*Turns up to*

opening and back, mopping head.) There's only one thing they're good for—to be mothers and bear boys.

ARAMINTA. Ah, that's the way you silly old bachelors talk! Naught else for us to do but to bear boys?

ASH. Naught else—except to bear girls. Women be wanted for the next generation. They ain't no manner of use to their own. I'm ashamed of Samuel Sweetland going round the country offering himself at sale prices. (*Crosses* L.) Everybody's talking about and making fun of him. (*By window* L.) 'Tis a disgrace to us males that he can sink to go among 'em hat in hand—only to get laughed at for his pains. (*Looks out of window up* L)

SIBLEY. Whatever are you saying?

ARAMINTA (*frowning and shaking her head at* ASH). Don't ask him—a sour old curmudgeon. He hates the women. You'll hear no good of us from him. (*Puts pail back under window.*)

(ASH *comes down to fireplace.*)

(*A knock at the door* R. SIBLEY, *who is making her apple-pie, goes to the door, wiping her hands, and admits* GEORGE SMERDON, *who goes to* R. *top corner of table.* SIBLEY *returns to behind table and finishes making her pie.*)

GEORGE (*to* SIBLEY). Morning! (*To* ARAMINTA.) Morning! When do you start for the station, Churdles?

ASH. In quarter of an hour.

GEORGE (*standing* R. *level with the table*). I'll drive down along with you, if you please. (*Puts hat on table, draws chair back a bit and sits* R. *of table.*)

(ASH *takes down a whip from above fireplace.*)

ARAMINTA (*rises*). So you shall then (*pointing to* ASH), and try tò make him see a bit of sense, George. (*Picks up her basin and the saucepan with potatoes.*) Come on, Ash—I want you afore you start. (*Crosses down towards door* R , *puts basin on dresser, opens door, picks up basin, and exit* R. *door, leaving same open.*)

ASH (*examining whip*). I be going to put the hoss in now. (*Then walks across, puts on hat, exit with whip, closing door.*)

GEORGE. Well, I went down

SIBLEY (*behind table*). So I hear, George.

GEORGE (*spreading out his legs in front of him*) Yes, to Dawlish I went, and had two walks with her. Once we tramped along by the sea, and once we went up over the moor. Walked her off her legs, I did. Pretty hopeful—eh?

SIBLEY. Yes, but——

GEORGE. And she likewise accepted a bag of prawns—a good sign that?

SIBLEY. Was she cheerful?

GEORGE. No, (*shaking his head*) I wouldn't say she was cheerful

—no more was your father. He said a lot of harsh things against the *women*, and Petronell had her knife into the *men*. They be such clever people. But the cleverest people ain't always clever enough to be happy.

SIBLEY. That's one thing makes it worth while being a fool, George. You can be happy, whatever else you can't be.

GEORGE. Not always. Look at me.

SIBLEY. You're no fool.

GEORGE. First cousin to it; and yet by no means happy. But I'm fighting every inch of the way—I'm hanging on like a bulldog, Sibley. I've got my teeth in her, you may say. (*Takes a whelk shell from his side pocket and holds it up in his left hand to* SIBLEY.) Do 'e see that shell?

SIBLEY. Yes.

GEORGE. 'Tis a whelk as I catched when we was walking over the rocks at low tide. (*Looking lovingly at it, holds it up in his* R *hand.*) And I had it cooked, and your sister was so terrible kind as to eat it. I shall keep that shell to my dying day.

(SIBLEY *has finished making her pie and is clearing up, wiping the flour off table, etc*)

SIBLEY. I know you care a lot for her.

GEORGE. She's everything—everything in the world.

SIBLEY. I wish I could help you

GEORGE. I wish you could. Nobody can help me. (*Puts shell in his left breast pocket.*) 'Tis a job have got to be done single-handed. I'm at it night and day, you might say—except when I'm asleep. How my brain stands it, I don't know, but I go battling on.

(*Enter* CHURDLES ASH *door down* R. *He just opens door, keeps his hand on handle.*)

ASH Here's Dick Coaker looking for Dr. Rundle and can't find him

(*Enter* RICHARD COAKER.)

(ASH *closes door, as he goes out again.*)

RICHARD. Morning, Sibley! (*Hangs up hat on peg below door* R. *and goes to dresser.*)

GEORGE. He's out with the hounds in his pink coat. I see him and Mrs. Windeatt and Valiant Dunnybrig and a score more riding to the meet.

SIBLEY (*taking the pie and implements from table*) Dr. Rundle, what's wrong? (*Looking at* RICHARD, *alarmed*)

RICHARD (*smiling reassuringly*). Only about some hay my old man sold him when he was at Miss Tapper's flare-up.

(SIBLEY *taking up tray with pie, etc., moving to* L.)

Don't you go, Sibley, please.

SIBLEY (*crossing round* L. *end of table to door* R.). I'll be back in a minute if you want me.

(RICHARD *opens door for her and closes it after her.*)

(GEORGE *and* RICHARD *look at each other in doubt.* GEORGE *shows the more feeling, puffs his cheeks and gets red, facing to* L.)

RICHARD (R). Fine day, George Smerdon.

GEORGE. I don't want no words with you, Richard Coaker. 'Tis very certain us can't be friends—so we'd better keep clear of each other till the battle's won, or lost.

RICHARD (*coming up* R.). And why the mischief can't we be friends, George ?

GEORGE. Because we can't.

RICHARD (*goes to dresser*). Been to Dawlish, I hear ?

GEORGE (*turning to* RICHARD). Yes, I did go to Dawlish But you didn't—that's one up against you, be sure of that.

RICHARD (R.). Why the devil should I go to Dawlish ? (*Looking out of window* R.)

GEORGE. What a question ! What's the good o' talking ? Ain't we bitter as death for the same woman ?

RICHARD. Good Lord ! (*He turns and goes behind* GEORGE *to back of table, stops and looks at him in astonishment.*) You don't want her, too ?

GEORGE. With every drop of blood I want her. Like a tiger I want her ; and your love-making, so to call it, is the moon to my sun. A bird in the hedge makes better love than you. To let her go out of your sight for a week and never to cross the road after her ! Call that love !

RICHARD (*he goes to* L. *of table and sits*). Man alive, she wasn't at Dawlish !

GEORGE. Wasn't at Dawlish ! (*Taking shell from pocket.*) Didn't I catch this whelk with these hands out of a pool at her feet ; and didn't I have it cooked for her ; and didn't she eat it ? I dare say you'd like that shell ! You'd have to kill me first, Richard Coaker, afore you'd get it ! (*Shows whelk-shell and returns it to his inside pocket.*)

RICHARD (*contemptuously*) That was only Petronell, George.

GEORGE. " Only Petronell." (*He sits bolt upright in his chair.*) Only Petronell !

RICHARD. Good Lord ! Are you chattering about her ?

GEORGE. And who else on the face of the earth be there to chatter about ?

RICHARD (*with a broad, pleasant smile*). My dear man, I haven't got no use for Petronell.

GEORGE Then why the mischief be you always dogging her footsteps ? Why be you always at Applegarth ? Why are you up here now, waiting for her to come back and too slack to go to the station to meet her and help with the parcels like I shall?

RICHARD (*still with a broad, happy smile*). Fancy you thinking that!

GEORGE. 'Tisn't only me; everybody thinks it.

RICHARD. Who?

GEORGE. Her father thinks it, for he told me so, and Miss Dench thinks it—(*he gets quite animated*)—and that slip of a girl Sibley thinks it, and—and she thinks it herself, for that matter.

RICHARD. I don't want Petronell, and never did want her. (*Rises, crosses and stands with back to fire.*)

GEORGE (*rises, pushes chair under table, spits on hands—puts on hat*). Then the sooner she knows it the better. And to-day she shall know it.

RICHARD (*on rug*). I'm after somebody else, and always have been.

GEORGE. Bah! There ain't anybody else.

(*Enter* SIBLEY *from* R., *followed by* CHURDLES ASH *with whip, who holds door open.* SIBLEY *crosses to front of dresser drawer.*)

ASH. Come on, George! I'm off.

(*Exit* CHURDLES ASH, *leaving door open.*)

RICHARD. Good luck, George!

GEORGE. She hasn't got a leg to stand upon now, that I can see.

(*Crosses towards door with determination.*)

RICHARD. You hunt her down, then.

(*Exit* GEORGE *after* ASH *and closes door.*)

SIBLEY. Poor George!

RICHARD. Rich George!

(SIBLEY *takes the coloured tablecloth from the dresser, shutting drawer, and proceeds to spread it on the table, having shifted chair* R *up a bit out of her way.*)

SIBLEY. 'Tis to be very poor to love a girl that don't love you, Richard.

RICHARD. Yes. (*Crosses to chair* L. *of table*) Not the only one in that fix

SIBLEY (*laughing. Throws cloth*). Easier to know your trouble than your luck, seemingly.

RICHARD. I'm glad I met George.

(SIBLEY *is* R. *of table.* RICHARD L. *of table, he makes an attempt to help with the cloth, but only succeeds in holding it up out of position.*)

I've told him something that have put life into him.

SIBLEY. I wish for Petronell's sake you could be a bit more like other people.

(*He is still rather hindering with the cloth.*)

Excuse my plain speaking. But—but—you'd better be off after Dr. Rundle.

RICHARD. I don't want him. (*Laughing at* SIBLEY.) 'Twas only an excuse to come up here

SIBLEY (*looking wistfully at* RICHARD) She ain't home yet.

RICHARD. Oh yes, she is.

SIBLEY. I ought to know.

RICHARD. So you ought, sure enough

SIBLEY. Why didn't you go to Dawlish? (*She sits chair* R. *end of table*)

RICHARD. Why should I? 'Twas only Petronell there. (*Casually.*)

SIBLEY. "Only Petronell!"

RICHARD. "Only Petronell!" You're as bad as George Smerdon.

SIBLEY. What more do you want than Petronell?

RICHARD. I'll tell you. (*Sits* L.C., *chair behind table. Pauses.*) I'm here to tell you afore they come home. (*Fiddling with cloth. Quietly*) I suppose a little quiet maiden like you be dazzled by Petronell, same as George Smerdon and a good few other folks. They can't imagine a man liking a nightingale *better* than a peacock

SIBLEY. She's not a peacock.

RICHARD. Leave her. It seems that your father and Miss Dench, and a fool here and there, all thought I came to Applegarth after your sister.

SIBLEY. Naturally. Who was there to come for else? Dear Petronell thought——

RICHARD. The same. I know But why? I never said a word—I never looked a word—I never squeezed her hand even. But because—(*tenderly*)—I was dumb and stupid as a pig along with you, and gay and easy along with her, they thought . . . there —it shows how a man may be misread. And that's why—(*happy thought*)—when Petronell appeared you was always off like a shot out of a gun, I suppose?

SIBLEY. Two's company, Richard.

RICHARD. And damn bad company if they're the wrong 'uns. 'Twas because you always bolted when you got half a chance that I hung fire

SIBLEY. I thought you came for her sake.

RICHARD I came for my own—and—(*tenderly*)—for hope to please you, Sibley.

SIBLEY (*after a bewildered look at him*). What a staggering thing!

(*In a low voice.*) I've always been wishful to befriend you—with Petronell!

RICHARD (*cheerily*) And little knew the thoughts I thought—and the cusses I cussed.

SIBLEY. This be treason to sister. (*Shaking her head sadly.*)

RICHARD (*bluff and cheerful*). Don't say that. (*Rises. He comes closer to her at back of table.*) She'll understand, if George can make her. George always says what he means, whatever his faults. He'll worry her now like a terrier worries a rat. (*Lightly.*) And oh, Sib—(*tenderly*)—I do love you so, dear—wrapped up in the very shadow of you, Sib. (*Whimsically.*) I've kissed the chair you sat on afore to-day. I have! A good year and more it have been going on now. (*He leans on table near to* SIBLEY. *Slowly.*) When d'you think it began?

SIBLEY. I don't know, Richard.

RICHARD (*looking in front*). In church. I happened to pitch alongside you, and you offered me a share of your hymn-book; and when I see your little thumb—(*looking at thumb*)—alongside my great big one—'twas a most touching sight and I never got over it. (*Holds up his* R. *thumb.*)

(SIBLEY *puts up hers, he laughs. Pause. She thinks—remembers perfectly; a happy smile, and a great light comes over her face. She speaks, with almost a sob in her voice.*)

SIBLEY. Your thumb was grubby, I remember.

RICHARD. God forgive me—(*laughing*)—I dare say it was.

SIBLEY (*gets up, very thoughtful, goes round front of table and ends speech between table and fire, facing* RICHARD, *almost back to audience*). I'm thinking on my sister. (L.C.) This is a fearful thing, Dick.

RICHARD (*brightly*). Think on me—I ain't a fearful thing. (*Going towards her round behind table.*) I'm the proudest man in Little Silver. (*Putting chair under* L. *end of table—stands below* L. *end of table.*)

SIBLEY (L.C.). I haven't took you yet.

RICHARD (*tenderly—moves* C. *by* L. *slowly*). Come here, you dinky dear! Come in my arms! (*Opening his arms, he stands close to her. She looks at him, but doesn't move.*) 'Tis all right with Petronell. She'll hate me for a minute and then she'll calm down. George be worth fifty of me.

SIBLEY (*putting her left hand on his arm*). Don't say that.

RICHARD. In cash—that's all. I'm so good as him in every other way. And Petronell's only got to think it over, then she'll understand. Wasn't her fault. 'Twas yours, and your father's, and 'Minta's.

(*Pause.*)

SIBLEY. When she knows you love *me*—oh dear!

(*Slowly she raises her eyes and looks into his, then buries her face on his shoulder. She is on his* L. *He puts his arm round her very gently. He makes no attempt to raise her head or to kiss her.*)

RICHARD. I'll warrant she'll come well out of it. She's made of fine stuff. She likes George better than you guess. I saw her with him at Miss Tapper's party.

SIBLEY (*her head leaning against him, holding his coat with both hands, and looking down, not at him*). I never dreamed of this—I never looked so high as you.

RICHARD. I was pluckier, I did look so high as you, my pretty bird. But you seemed a terrible long way off—and yet here you be in my arms—and glad to be! Say you be glad. (*Pleadingly.*)

SIBLEY (*moving back from him a step and looking up into his face*). Is it right? Is it honest, Richard?

RICHARD (*a step to her, he takes her in his arms*). Honest as the sunshine. (*With face close to hers, her lips near his.*) Kiss me, for God's sake! (*They kiss, a long, silent, restful kiss.*) And loving me a little bit all the time, I'll swear. (*He holds her at arms' length, looking at her.*)

SIBLEY. I always loved you when I dared to think of you. I couldn't help it. But I wept salt tears for my wickedness when I did. (*Buries her face on his shoulder and smiles at him.* SIBLEY *is now on his* R *arm. He stoops over her.*)

RICHARD. Never let me see no tears on your face—(*with something between laughing and crying*)—else I'll lick 'em off. (*He holds her in his arms again.*)

(*They are kissing each other when* ARAMINTA *comes in door down* R.)

ARAMINTA. My gracious! (*Surprised, falling back, goes out again, closing door.*)

(*They remain with his arms round her quite still.* ARAMINTA *re-enters and closes door.*)

RICHARD (*triumphantly and cheerfully*). Don't go! Don't go! We ain't ashamed of it. (*They cross to* C.) Miss Dench!

SIBLEY (*running to* ARAMINTA R). Oh, 'Minta, 'Minta!—he came here for *me*, and he's offered and I've took him. For God's sake it ban't wicked to Petronell.

ARAMINTA. My dear—— (*Pause. Not quite recovered from her surprise. Then a look at* RICHARD, *then she wraps her up in a large-hearted loving embrace.*) My dear little Sibley! (*Pause. Complete change of tone over* SIBLEY's *shoulder.*) You crafty toad, Richard Coaker!

(*She leads* SIBLEY *to chair* R. *of table.* SIBLEY *sits.*)

RICHARD. I know it. Cunning as a bushel of snakes. But I've got her. She's caught. The storm have been brewing for a month o' Sundays, Miss Dench, and now it's busted. (*He sits* L. *of table and leans over it.*)

ARAMINTA. A lot of blind sillies we've been! (*Is back of table.*) If us didn't all think—goodness knows why—— (*Sits.*)

RICHARD. If you'd only let me alone to mind my own business; but you was always heaving t'other girl at my head.

SIBLEY. Am I right, 'Minta?

ARAMINTA. Of course you're right. We were wrong—not you

SIBLEY. I was always terribly addicted to Richard.

RICHARD (*with a quiet, happy laugh*). And so you always ran away from me, as if I was the plague in a pair o' boots. (*He gets up and goes in front of table to* R) I'm off now.

SIBLEY (*coming down and catching him on her* R., *standing up and holding him*). Don't you go—'tis you must break it to father. I don't dare.

RICHARD. I'll break it to him fast enough. (*Taking her in his arms again.*) Never fear for that. I'll just run across and tell Uncle Henry—then I'll come back. 'Twill be meat and drink to Uncle Henry. He's awful fond of you. (*Tenderly*)

(*Another embrace.*)

SIBLEY. Don't be long, then. I can't bear you out of my sight now.

RICHARD. I'll never be out o' your sight no more, very soon. (*He goes to kiss her.*)

(SIBLEY *looks round at* ARAMINTA, *who hastily looks the other way as he goes off. She lingeringly keeps hold of his hand and goes with him to door—exit* RICHARD *and looks out after he has gone. She shuts the door very slowly, with a look of happy wonder on her face.*)

(ARAMINTA *goes* L. *of table to the front of it, and stands there with her arms spread out* L C. *She does not speak till* SIBLEY *has come to her and she has kissed her.*)

ARAMINTA. My own little pet! Oh, I'm so glad for 'e! 'Tis a brave, bright bit o' news. 'Twill cheer up father.

SIBLEY. But Petronell?

ARAMINTA. She'll know where she is now.

SIBLEY. But Petronell——

ARAMINTA. She won't want him no more. 'Twas only his holding off made her so coming on.

(*A knock at the door* R. ARAMINTA *answers it, going in front of* SIBLEY, *who remains just where she is, looking towards door*)

(*Enter* MISS THIRZA TAPPER)

MISS TAPPER. Good morning, Araminta! Good morning,

Sibley! (*She comes in front of* ARAMINTA *and shakes hands with* SIBLEY C.) You expected me? You had my postcard?

(ARAMINTA *closes door, goes to back of table*)

SIBLEY. So I had—(*she looks round at the postcard, which is standing up on the mantelshelf*)—and quite forgot it, Miss Tapper! The harvest decorations?

MISS TAPPER (*goes* R *of table*) Your dear father promised me quantities of laurel and yew. I have come in the Vicar's pony carriage to fetch it (*Sits* R. *end of table*)

SIBLEY (*still standing leaning in front of table* L.C. *of same*). So you shall, Miss Tapper. Churdles Ash will be back from the station directly. You shall choose what you want. (*Front corner of table* L.C.)

ARAMINTA (*back of table* R. *end of same*). I hope you've quite got over it, miss, and feel none the worse?

MISS TAPPER. My little affair? I've not got over it at all. It was a terrible strain—(*turns to* ARAMINTA)—so very much seemed to happen in such a short space of time—that outrageous person. I shall never forgive myself.

(*Voices heard outside.*)

SWEETLAND (*off* R. *in an angry voice*) Damn it, Ash, you get clumsier every day of your life!

SIBLEY. There's father!

ARAMINTA (*back of table*). He's come! Master's home again! (*Puts* C. *chair under table.*)

MISS TAPPER Then perhaps I may get the opportunity to say a few words of explanation to dear Mr Sweetland. I owe it to him. (*Rises.*)

(*The door* R *is thrown open.* SAMUEL SWEETLAND *enters first.* PETRONELL *comes next. She kisses* ARAMINTA, *who goes behind her round to* R. *of* SWEETLAND *to help him with coat, etc.* PETRONELL *goes behind table to armchair above fireplace.* CHURDLES ASH *follows them in with two parcels and two portmanteaux, puts them ready up stage* C. *to be taken into house.*)

SWEETLAND (*obviously in a bad temper. Seeing* MISS TAPPER, *he pulls up short*). You! (*He turns to* SIBLEY *who has come over to him*) Ah, Sibley! (*Kisses her.*)

(SIBLEY *goes over to* PETRONELL *and kisses her.* MISS TAPPER *crosses to* L. *end of table.* SWEETLAND *hangs up his hat, then goes to* ARAMINTA, *who helps him off with his coat and examines button.*)

PETRONELL (*listlessly*) Here we are (*Kisses* SIBLEY, *who has crossed and is between* PETRONELL *and* MISS TAPPER)

SWEETLAND (*to* ARAMINTA). What's Tapper doing here?

SIBLEY. Miss Tapper's come about the green stuff for the decorations.

(SIBLEY *puts her in armchair.* ARAMINTA *hangs coat on hook below door.*)

SWEETLAND (*coming down* R.). Pity you couldn't choose a more fitting time.

MISS TAPPER. Oh . . . if this is not the right moment . . . (*Crosses to* SWEETLAND C.)

SWEETLAND. I wish I knew the right moment. I haven't found it yet. (*Turns up* R.)

(MISS TAPPER *crosses to* R.C.)

ASH (*takes hat off*). 'Tis the right moment for clipping the yew hedge, and if you'll come along, miss, I'll do it now afore dinner. (*Comes to* R. *end of table.*)

(ARAMINTA *crosses up and carries one portmanteau and parcel upstairs through door* L.)

MISS TAPPER. Thank you, Mr. Ash. (ASH *follows* ARAMINTA *with the other two. She stands still.*)

(SWEETLAND *looks at her with a* "*why don't you go?*" *expression, crosses up* R. *by dresser.*)

SIBLEY (*to* PETRONELL, *alone, in an undertone*). Petronell dear, come in the garden a minute before you take off your jacket—such a wonderful thing!

(PETRONELL *rises and goes towards garden door.*)

I want to tell you first of all Have you seen George?

PETRONELL (*stops*). Have I seen George! When do I see anybody but George? I wish some other people were as much in earnest as that fellow.

(*During this* SWEETLAND *takes lozenge-box from his pocket.*)

SIBLEY. Perhaps they are.

(*Exeunt* SIBLEY *and* PETRONELL *through* R.C. *door into garden, closing it*)

(ASH *returns from door up* L. SWEETLAND *crosses to* ASH, *who is* L C. *at back*)

SWEETLAND (*to* ASH). Cut her a dollop of evergreens and send her going. (*He crosses* L., *puts box of lozenges on mantelpiece*)

(MISS TAPPER *is still standing* R.C, *fiddling with her bag.*)

ASH (*puts on hat. Goes to garden door* R C., *opens it and returns* C)
Come on, miss.

Miss Tapper. Thank you, Mr. Ash. (*Turns up* R C.) The Vicar's pony carriage is at the gate.

(*Exit* Churdles Ash, *garden door.*)

(Sweetland *is* L. *He turns and looks at* Miss Tapper, *and listens to her with no expression on his face*)

(*To* Sweetland) Shall see you again, dear Mr. Sweetland.

(Sweetland *grunts.*)

(*Exit* Miss Tapper, *by garden door, which she leaves open.*)

(Araminta *enters, shuts the garden door after* Miss Tapper. *When* Sweetland *sits in armchair by fire, she comes and stands on his* R.)

Sweetland (*having put his box of jujubes on the extreme upper end of the mantelpiece, moves armchair down by chair* L. *and sits*). That woman have no feeling for time or place! Well, 'tis all over, 'Minta. The game's up—I'm broken—I'm done for. (*Takes paper out of his pocket.*) That's the last of 'em. (*Scratches his pencil through list.*)

Araminta. Don't talk like that—a brave creature like you. (*She sits* L. *of table.*)

Sweetland. Truth's truth, and I see it all. The whole power of the female sex be drawn up against me. Some enemy's put the evil eye on me, I believe—else it couldn't be they all. . . . 'Tis very bad for one's character. My self-respect have gone.

Araminta. Don't you say that, Sweetland. I won't hear a strong sensible man like you say that.

Sweetland. It's hit me hard—cruel hard.

Araminta. Make light of it, my dear, and look forward.

Sweetland. If you make light of your misfortunes, everybody else be only too darned glad to do the same. I won't make light of it. 'Tisn't a light matter.

Araminta (*gently leading him to the subject she wishes to hear about*). Mrs. Mercy Bassett didn't see her way?

Sweetland. 'Twas touch and go. I thought I'd got her. It shaped all right, though she's aged a good bit since I last saw her. I felt thankful for small mercies and went at her in a humble spirit.

Araminta. What was her objection?

Sweetland. She couldn't tell me. She is one of they maddening women who can't make up their mind. I spent a good bit of money one way and another. I took her up to Exeter for a treat, and showed her the cathedral and the museum. She liked they Egyptian mummies at the museum far better than the cathedral. A morbid woman. I was generous, 'Minta, and gave her a bottle of sherry wine with her dinner. Cost four bob it did.

Araminta. Who could do more?

SWEETLAND. *And* she drank it, and instead of lifting her up, it cast her down

ARAMINTA. What a pity! It do with some people.

SWEETLAND She liked my appearance and manners and ways and gift of speech

ARAMINTA. Of course she did.

SWEETLAND But she was afraid of leaving the seaside, because of a catch in her breathing-parts It takes her of a night.

ARAMINTA. Dartmoor air be the best in the world.

SWEETLAND. So I told her. I listened to all her silly objections and didn't show so much as a pinch of temper.

ARAMINTA I'm sure you didn't.

SWEETLAND. But she broke me down at last. (*Testily*) I got full up with cranks and whimsies, and the manhood flashed out in me, and I told her I was off. (*He gets up and stands back to fireplace*) I also told her that she might go to hell for a husband (*Turns up to window* L. *in front of armchair and down again behind it*)

ARAMINTA. Oh dear!—'twas all over then, of course?

SWEETLAND (*down* L C., *turning and facing* ARAMINTA). Far from it My language braced her up. She very near flung herself into my arms. Then she relapsed and wept a bucket.

(*He has taken his pipe from pocket, and looked round on shelf. She goes over to dresser, gets a box of matches from drawer, comes to* R *of table*)

This morning she was at the station She brought a nosegay of roses as a parting gift Looking back, I'm glad she said "no." She's too weak and floppy I'd be the oak to any woman's ivy in reason, but she'd choke me I want a woman, not a jelly-fish.

ARAMINTA. You poor man! (*Sits on chair end of table and picks up matches. Lights his pipe.*) 'Tis enough to weaken your faith in the whole pack of us

SWEETLAND. No—I don't say that no more. I'm a difficult man. I'm very low-spirited about it. I don't much want to go on living, 'Minta, if I'm to be wed no more.

ARAMINTA You must pull yourself together. There's as good and better than these.

SWEETLAND. I know it—that's the hard thing. I'm far too sensible to pretend there ain't plenty of proper women wandering about and open to a fair offer. But I've had my share. I've had my Tibby. I shall never get another now.

ARAMINTA. I'll wager there's a fine useful creature waiting for you yet. You'll have a splendid triumph the very next time, I shouldn't wonder.

SWEETLAND. I've got a lot of faults. (*Puts matches in pocket.*) The truth is that I've been thinking too much of myself—not enough about other people.

ACT III.] THE FARMER'S WIFE. 89

ARAMINTA. We all do. 'Tis human nature to put ourselves first.

SWEETLAND You don't 'Twas you opened my eyes to it. You put everybody else first Your——

ARAMINTA. Don't waste time praising me—I'm nobody. (*Crosses to dresser and gets pad.*) Let's think what to do next.

SWEETLAND. You may be a nobody, but you're a good Christian nobody, 'Minta, and a proper big-hearted nobody.

ARAMINTA (*comes to* C. *back of table. Brings paper, pad, and pencil. Reflecting and not heeding him*). Have you ever thought about that nice woman Jane Cherry, the huckster's sister ? (*She sits back of table*)

SWEETLAND. No, I haven't, and I ain't going to. What's Jane Cherry to me ? Listen, 'Minta. Confession is good for the soul. I have seen all my silly faults very clear of late. There's no place like the lonely seashore to show you what a poor thing you are. But you be a steadfast glass in which a man may see the truth of himself if he's minded to.

ARAMINTA Never mind that I be proud to be useful to you and yours in my small way. And I hope you'll always let me. Jane Cherry——

SWEETLAND. Araminta, list to me. I be sudden and rash as usual, for what I'm going to say only come over me in the train an hour ago But there is a *woman*—one woman——

ARAMINTA. I'm glad to hear you say that. I'll help you heart and soul, if 'tis in my power to do so.

SWEETLAND. 'Tis in your power, no doubt. (*Gets up and stands back to fireplace again at the lower end.*) But what will you say when I tell you her name ? You'll say, " Here's a man as be offering second-hand goods."

ARAMINTA. Don't matter a button what I'd say. Who is she ? If she's clever and sensible, she wouldn't say that—even if she knew your misfortunes.

SWEETLAND (*advancing*). Let me speak. I'm not talking about any other woman ; I'm talking about you. If I'd come to you first I should have been a wise man. A very poor figure I cut, no doubt —like a storm-foundered ship trying to beat into harbour afore she sinks And why such a rare piece as you should—

(*He has a fit of coughing.*)

(*She gets lozenges from extreme upper end of mantelshelf and hands them to him on his* R. *hand and puts box back on shelf after he has taken one and goes to back of table* C.)

—be a blessed harbour—for me, be blessed if I know. (*Clears his throat. Takes lozenge.*) So there 'tis. My eyes are open and I see that while I was climbing the hedge, the flower was at my feet. And I do believe—I do humbly believe——

(*She takes pad and pencil back to dresser and comes on his* R. *in front of table.*)

But stop me if you've heard too much. Don't think you'll make me angry if you say "no." I'm tamed to hear "no" I expect "no." I don't see how you can well say anything else to such a man. But I'd like to mention one thing in my favour, 'Minta. A little child can lead me——

ARAMINTA (*on his* R., *looks up into his face and smiles*) I know that.

SWEETLAND. I grant there haven't been much signs of it lately; but I be only waiting for your hand.

ARAMINTA. You'd wed me, Samuel Sweetland?

SWEETLAND. That would I, Araminta, and do my mightiest to be worthy. Not good enough by a thousand miles—though I may have been for the others—*quite* good enough for them. But not for you. 'Tis like the starling offering to wed the golden plover—me offering for you. You're a wonder and I'm a scorn

ARAMINTA. No wonder me, and no scorn you. Just an everyday man and woman, no better nor worse than their neighbours I've known you for a real good chap many a year now.

SWEETLAND. If you've seen the best of me, 'Minta, you've seen the worst But bad's the best. No, I don't deserve one *kind word* from you. I deserve naught—yet ask all

ARAMINTA Be sure you mean this? (*Sits* L. *end of table.*) 'Tis fearful sudden.

SWEETLAND. Like all conversions. (*Pulls armchair round and sits close to her.*) The Lord works same as the lightning, and don't give warning where He's going to strike and wake sense in a man's heart. And I'm not too old to mend. I may even rise up to be good enough for such a gracious woman as you Such charity as you've got covers a multitude of sins, 'Minta. Can it cover mine? (*He puts out his hands to her.*)

(*A pause.*)

No—I reckon it can't. I'm sorry. I'm asking too much. Forgive me

ARAMINTA. I'll take you, Samuel

SWEETLAND. You mean it?

ARAMINTA. I mean it. 'Tis a solemn and great uplifting. But if you can rise to it, so can I. Us knows each other's tempers very well—our strength and our weakness—and give and take be the whole art of marriage, so far as I can see from the outside. (*Gives him her hand.*) I'll enter in, Samuel, I'll enter in with trust and hope —and proud to enter in along with such a man as you.

(SWEETLAND *rises, standing on her* L., *and holding her hand. She looks up in his face.*)

SWEETLAND. You're a blessed pattern of woman, you be—light in the world's twilight, the likes of you, and always have been. And if you repent this day's work, then may I lose my salvation. (*Hand on* ARAMINTA'S L. *shoulder.*)

ARAMINTA (*laughing*). 'Twill be a shattering surprise for your maidens.

SWEETLAND (*goes behind table to* C. *of it*). Brave news for them and all the world. And now—now this minute—to mark the change, you must blossom out afore them, same as the sun from behind a cloud. You must go a lot finer from this hour—from this very hour.

ARAMINTA. Churdles Ash says that we change our clothes—not our claws.

SWEETLAND. None ever saw your claws; and none ever saw you in clothes worth the name.

ARAMINTA. Mercy me! What about my Sundays?

SWEETLAND. 'Tis only one sad-coloured gown instead of another. Now list what you must do. Afore my dear Tibby went she'd laid in a brave, flame-new, party dress, and never once wore it.

ARAMINTA. She did, for Jane Westaway's wedding she bought it.

SWEETLAND. And went to wear her heavenly robes afore the day came.

ARAMINTA. And she wished for me to have the new frock—bade me take it. 'Twould fit me proper, she said.

SWEETLAND. But you never wore it?

ARAMINTA. Good powers, no! 'Tis much too fine.

SWEETLAND. You get into they clothes this moment. (*Goes up a bit and turns.*) I order you, 'Minta. And deck your hair a trifle more dashing too.

ARAMINTA. I can't, Samuel—I don't know how.

SWEETLAND. There's nothing you couldn't do if you try—(*comes down to table with a change of tone, in a softer voice*)—nothing you wouldn't do to please me. I be going to do countless rare things to pleasure you, 'Minta—thousands of 'em—so just this one—now—quick, afore Tapper goes. 'Twill be such a noble sight for her to report in the parish.

ARAMINTA. Fancy my looking at myself in the glass!

SWEETLAND. You'll see something as will astonish you. So set about it.

(*Enter* CHURDLES ASH *through garden door, in his shirt-sleeves, with a faggot of green stuff, which he puts down near dresser, and clear of door, leaving garden door open.*)

(*To* ASH.) Where's Sibley?

ASH (R.C). She's down in the garden along with old Tapper.

SWEETLAND. We mustn't let Miss Tapper go for a minute.

There's news flying about yet. (*To* ARAMINTA) Don't you forget now. I be set on it. I will have it so.

(*Exit* SWEETLAND, *gaily laughing by garden door* R.C., *which he closes.*)

(ARAMINTA *sits staring before her and takes no notice of* ASH.)

ASH. There—though why the Almighty should like for our hedge-clippings to go into His holy house, I can't see. (*Takes hat—up at back.*) What's happened? You've got him into a good temper again. (*Shaking his head*) You always do.

ARAMINTA. I hope I always shall. (*Rises, stands* L C., *looking towards fireplace, back to* ASH.)

ASH (*looks at her, then at the audience—comes down a little* R. *of table*). 'Tis only because you agree with him. You ought to withstand him more.

(*She laughs shyly, facing to fireplace.*)

ARAMINTA. The master's going to wed in earnest.
ASH. Never! Catched that woman to Dawlish after all?
ARAMINTA. Catched a woman, but not to Dawlish.
ASH. God befriend me and you then. (*Turns up* R) To think of another female in this house!
ARAMINTA. She's no stranger, Churdles (*Walks down* L C.)
ASH (*comes down*). From this place?
ARAMINTA. Yes; a common, everyday object, you might say. (*Turns round and faces him.*) In fact, I be the woman, Churdles Ash
ASH (*drops cap, indicating utmost astonishment. Points*). You! (*Sniffing and picking up cap—sniff again.*) Go on!
ARAMINTA. Solemn truth. He's offered and I was proud to answer "yes."
ASH. Jimmery! (*Sitting* R. *of table, accepting the fact. Pauses, mopping his head, after throwing his cap on table*) Well, they say as the next best thing to no wife be a good one. He's come out top at last.
ARAMINTA. 'Tis a great advancement for a simple creature like me.
ASH (*points*). I'll be on your side. I'll help you with the man.
ARAMINTA. I know you will.
ASH. Yes—sense alive you'll find me (*Spits on hands.*) If I had a threepenny piece for every bit of sense I speak, I'd be so rich as George Smerdon this minute. You'll get to his ear now. Don't you forget to tell him I'm cruel underpaid, 'Minta. But there—(*with a slightly sarcastic laugh*)—of course you'll be the "Missis" in future (*picks up hat*) and "'Minta" no more (*Puts hat on.*)

(*A knock at the door.*)

ARAMINTA (*going towards the door* R. *and stops* C.). 'Twill make no difference at all, Churdles Ash.

ASH (*grunts. Rises*) You wait till you feel the whip in your hand and find yourself reigning over us! (*Going up* R.) I dare say you'll be a proper slave-driver then and, (*at door*) instead of doing other people's work, you'll make 'em do yours.

(*Exit* ASH *door* R.C *into garden, shutting door*)

(ARAMINTA *opens* R *door.* MARY HEARN *enters—stands by door.*)

ARAMINTA. Mary!

MARY. To see dear Mr Sweetland.

ARAMINTA. You are a stranger! (*Closing door and going up* R.C.) Yes, he's in. I'll tell him.

(*Enter* SWEETLAND *from garden door* R.C., *which he closes.*)

SWEETLAND What did I tell you, 'Minta?

ARAMINTA (L.C.). I know. I ain't forgot.

(*Exit* L *up steps to change her dress.*)

SWEETLAND (*down* L.C. *Moves chair to fireplace*) And what might you want, Miss Hearn?

MARY (*crosses to* L. *of table*). Speak kindly. Forget the past, dear Mr. Sweetland.

SWEETLAND. I'm going to—just so quick as ever I can—be sure o' that.

MARY. Call me Mary.

SWEETLAND (*starts*). You don't mean?

MARY. I've brought cruel bad news for you. A telegram. I took it off the wires myself, and I wouldn't have nobody else see it, so I carried it up. The lady at Dawlish—Mrs. Mercy Bassett. She's changed her mind about you. There's no Mercy for you in that quarter, poor man (*Gives him a telegram.*)

SWEETLAND. What the mischief do you mean?

(*Crosses* R., *throwing envelope down on table by* MARY)

MARY. She's changed her mind—that's all. You think you're engaged to be married?

SWEETLAND. And if I do?

MARY. Well—you ain't; she's gone back on you.

SWEETLAND (*reading telegram*). "Have reconsidered my answer. Mercy." (*Sits* R. *of table. Laughs.*)

MARY. But don't you mind, Samuel. (*Facing him, and rather leaning over table.*) There was one you wanted more than Mercy Bassett—not so long ago. And if this here widow can change her mind, because she's a fool, somebody else can because she's a wise woman.

SWEETLAND But you don't understand, Mary. (*Flourishing telegram.*) This means——

MARY. Never mind what it means. Just you throw your memory back to Tapper's tea-party, and what I did and said. It was her beastly coffee upset my nerves. I turned you down and I'm sorry for it. Other people can reconsider their answers besides Mercy Bassett. Don't look at me like that—I'm all blushes, Samuel

SWEETLAND. Good powers! You want me?

MARY. I want to make you a happy man, if I can.

SWEETLAND. You have! You have, Mary.

MARY. Don't you speak all of a minute. Take your time.

(*Enter* MISS TAPPER *from garden door. Goes down* R)

SWEETLAND. You shall hear my answer afore you go.

MISS TAPPER (*down* R) Sibley thought I should find you alone now.

SWEETLAND (*staring at her*). My conscience, you too? (*Rises* L. *and crosses up to stairs.*) You ain't going to ... Just you wait here I want to tell Miss Dench something. Back in half a minute. (*Takes paper from pocket and scans it*) Things are looking up, ladies.

(*Exit* SWEETLAND *up steps* L., *waving paper.*)

MARY. Don't 'ee take no notice of him. He ain't quite himself· A bit light-headed. He's had an ugly knock—and then a bit of good news on top of it.

MISS TAPPER (*coming forward* R *by table*) I hope you've quite recovered, Mary, from that dreadful attack at my little affair?

MARY. It was something I ate.

(MISS TAPPER *is standing* R. *of table. Rather aloof from* MARY, *who is still seated* L. *of table.*)

MISS TAPPER (*stiffly*). It was certainly nothing you ate—unless you ate too much.

MARY (*laughs*). There wasn't no fear of that.

MISS TAPPER. Your nerves want attention, probably.

MARY. Yes, you often get weak nerves with extra good brains. But the dratted men are jealous of woman's intellects and keep us clever ones down. They're nasty wretches—men are—where women are concerned.

MISS TAPPER (*coming forward in front of table*). There are good and bad men.

MARY. Oh yes—there's good and bad. I know that quite as well as you do—perhaps better. I might have been a wife myself if I'd liked. I may be in a man's arms yet before I'm much older.

MISS TAPPER. Try to be more reticent and dignified. It's very vulgar to jest on such sacred things, even to a fellow-woman. (*She goes towards garden door, as if having decided to end the interview.*)

MARY. Hoity! Toity! Grapes are sour, perhaps. I'd like to see the man that wanted you, anyway. (*Picks up envelope.*) Nasty they may be, but they're not born fools.

MISS TAPPER (*after a painful but ineffectual effort to control herself, comes close to table* R *, back of it by chair* C*. She doesn't shout, but her voice vibrates with anger*). You low-minded wretch! You shameless minx! To think that a department of the Civil Service is in your hands!

(MARY *laughs.*)

But know this—if only in honour of my dear father's memory—I, too, might have been a wife—the wife of a high-minded and most worthy man.

MARY (*excited : tilting back her chair in a reckless way*). Easy to talk, but let's hear who 'twas. The Lord of the Manor, perhaps; or was it the Bishop of Exeter? They'd fly afore you—they'd call on the hills to cover 'em afore you—— (*Her excitement increases. She gets up and leans right over the table*) Thirza *Trapper* you ought to be called; but cunning though you may be, you'll never catch a man. Tell out his name and let's hear who went "nap" on you! Names, names, you pinnicking little grey rat! (*She sways forward at* MISS TAPPER, *then sits* L *of table again and begins to laugh very loud.*)

(*Enter* SIBLEY SWEETLAND *and* SAMUEL SWEETLAND *from up* L. *He comes behind table, a little* L. *and between them.* SIBLEY, *rather frightened, hangs back* R.C.)

SWEETLAND. Hallo! That laugh again!

MARY I'm only laughing at the Vicar's pet. Here's the men all running to marry her, she says. (*She laughs wildly.*)

SWEETLAND. Ladies! Ladies! Aren't you old enough to know better? (*He goes* L. *of table.*) Here, take Miss Hearn in the garden and give her a ripe pear, Sibley—

(MARY *rises.*)

—and calm her down. I've got something to tell her presently.

(MARY *goes up* L. *of chair where* SIBLEY *joins her at back, taking her arm*)

MARY. Ah! And don't you let Tabby Tapper go till she's heard it.

(*They go off into garden, closing door* R.C.)

MISS TAPPER. That outrageous woman, it's only charitable to assume she's mad.

SWEETLAND (*goes* L. *in front of table*). She's sane enough She's like a lot more ; she's found out which side her bread was buttered—too late.

MISS TAPPER (*she has got a little nearer gradually, moving in direction of* C *of table*). Oh, Mr. Sweetland, may I take this opportunity of telling you how bitterly I regretted . . .

SWEETLAND. Stop! Stop! There's a time for everything, Thirza, and when the time's passed it never comes back.

MISS TAPPER. Oh, but I merely meant——

SWEETLAND. I don't blame you—I don't blame anybody. (*Looking up from where he is, he can see through the window. He goes a little nearer to it to see more clearly.*) God's powers, if there ain't Widow Windeatt! (*Takes favourite position back to fire.*) Why, that's the whole boilin' of 'em! A proper man-hunt, this is!

(MISS TAPPER *goes to* R.)

(*Enter* VALIANT DUNNYBRIG, SIBLEY SWEETLAND, PETRONELL SWEETLAND, *and* LOUISA WINDEATT *by garden door, followed by* RICHARD COAKER LOUISA *follows with* SIBLEY *on her* L. *and* PETRONELL *on her* R. *They go to back of table.* MISS TAPPER, *at their entrance, stands back to audience, facing* LOUISA *down* R. DUNNYBRIG *comes down* R. *He and the widow are dressed in hunting attire, and she has evidently had a bad fall. She is smeared with earth, her face is dirty, her habit is torn, and her hat is crushed, but she is quite cheerful.* RICHARD *helps* LOUISA *into chair* C *of table and* PETRONELL *goes up to corner of dresser by window and places work-basket on window-sill.*)

```
         PETRONELL
            ●

           RICHARD  LOUISA  SIBLEY
              ●       ●       ●
         ┌─────────────────────┐
         │                     │
 DUNNYBRIG                     │
    ●    │                     │
         └─────────────────────┘

 ● MISS TAPPER                        SWEETLAND
                                          ●
```

DUNNYBRIG. Any port in a storm! Here's the poor dear been throwed over a hedge on Honeybag Down, and but for God's mercy must have broke her neck.

LOUISA. I'm all right Nothing's broke. 'Tis only a shake-up.

SIBLEY. Where's 'Minta, father?

SWEETLAND. Ah, 'tis always "Where's 'Minta ? " when man, woman or child's in trouble. Ever ready to spread her wings and fly to help But she's busy on my account just now. But a drink you must have.

(RICHARD, *assisted by* PETRONELL, *gets bottle and two glasses from dresser cupboard up* R RICHARD *comes to back of table and gives a glass to* MISS TAPPER, *which* SWEETLAND *fills*. PETRONELL *puts six glasses on tray and takes them* L. *to* SWEETLAND, *who fills them*. MISS TAPPER *comes* R. *of table*.)

All of you must drink. There's something to drink about, I promise you.

RICHARD (*at table*). That there is.

SWEETLAND. Now then, in the first place—(*pouring out cherry brandy*. MISS TAPPER *sips hers*) Ah! You've started, I see, Miss Tapper.

(MISS TAPPER *goes down* R. *again, and* DUNNYBRIG *goes up* R)

That's Miss Dench's cherry brandy, and you won't get better in this world—or the next.

(RICHARD, *back of table, gets a glass for* DUNNYBRIG, *who is up* R., *and himself*.)

Here's my Sibley hitched up to Dick Coaker for a start——

DUNNYBRIG. Well done, Dick ! Here's luck to the pair of 'e ! (*He drinks to* RICHARD.)

RICHARD. Thank ye—— (*Who has taken his own glass*)

(RICHARD *smiles pleasantly, nods his head and drinks. They all drink* PETRONELL *kisses* SIBLEY, *and goes up to window* L. *and puts her glass on the sill*. SIBLEY *puts her glass on* C. *table and crosses with* RICHARD *behind armchair to fireplace*. DUNNYBRIG *turns to speak to* MISS TAPPER, *between dresser and door* R)

SWEETLAND. Bless you both ! (*Drinks*.) But, you haven't heard what's happened to your father yet. Wonders in the land, I promise you.

(*Enter* HENRY COAKER, *followed by* CHURDLES ASH *and* MARY HEARN, *with apple, and* GEORGE SMERDON. MARY *goes to chair* R. *of table and sits*. HENRY, *with a sympathetic pat on the shoulder for* LOUISA, *comes to chair* L *of table and sits* GEORGE SMERDON, *with both hands in his pockets, dull and out of spirits, up* R. DUNNYBRIG *goes to* R. *by table* R. *of* LOUISA)

HENRY (*patting* LOUISA). Well, my dear, how be 'e after your fall ? (*Sits* L. *of table*.)

ASH (R C). The hoss be all right. He's as sorry for his sins as a hoss can be.

G

98   THE FARMER'S WIFE.   [ACT III.

(MARY HEARN *sits* R. *of table.* PETRONELL *comes down by table*
L.C. *at back.*)

SWEETLAND (*goes to table and passes* MARY *a glass*). Drink, Mary
Hearn; take your lap with the rest. (*Comes down* L.C.) The painful
truth is that a few of us—to name no names—have missed our
market during the last week or two. 'Twill be a lesson to the losers
to make up their minds a bit sharper another time.

PETRONELL (*she speaks rather hesitatingly*). George, come into
the garden. I've something to tell you. (*He crosses to her* R.)

(*Exeunt* PETRONELL *and* GEORGE *into garden, leaving door open*)

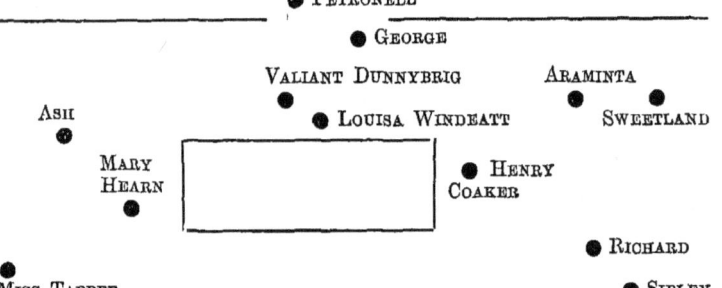

(*The company, except* SWEETLAND *and* SIBLEY, *exchange glances, and
look towards the garden door.*)

HENRY (*seated*). You don't sound like a defeated man, Sweetland.
MARY (*seated*). Tell 'em you're a conqueror, Samuel.
SWEETLAND (*goes behind table between* LOUISA *and old* HENRY).
I'm going to, Mary. I'm going to. Is everybody here? (*Goes to
door and shouts.*) Be you coming down house, Miss Dench? Ah,
here she is—like the Queen of Sheba!

(*Enter* ARAMINTA DENCH, *transformed. She wears rather a garish
gown and has made her hair look nice. She appears ten years
younger.*)

(*At* ARAMINTA'S *entrance, general surprise, and all look at her.*)

MISS TAPPER. A stranger?
ASH. Stranger be damned! 'Tis our Miss Dench.
SIBLEY. My darling 'Minta!

(RICHARD *and* SIBLEY *are near fireplace.* SWEETLAND *meets*
ARAMINTA *and puts his right arm round her waist.*)

SWEETLAND. Not "'Minta" to nobody but me. Not "darling"
to nobody but me. 'Tis Miss Araminta Dench of Applegarth
Farm, neighbours, and she's done me the honour . . . in a word . . -.

(MARY HEARN *screams and begins to gurgle.* DUNNYBRIG *soothes her and gives her some cherry brandy, and* CHURDLES ASH *fans her with his hat.* MISS TAPPER *puts her glass down on dresser.*)

HENRY (*seated* L. *of table*). No good, post-mistress
SWEETLAND. In a word, my wife to be. I'd have her know she wasn't the only one was willing. And if anybody knows a woman with a gentler heart, a straighter back and a nobler character, this side of Plymouth, I'll very much like to see her.

SIBLEY. They don't—they don't—father!

LOUISA (*seated* C.). That they don't!

HENRY (*gets up and pats* ARAMINTA *affectionately on the shoulder. He is now back to audience. He sees* GEORGE *and* PETRONELL *through door* R C., *toddles up to it*). A proper working Christian, as I've always said. (*Goes to porch opening.*)

MISS TAPPER. There's no one like Miss Dench.

SWEETLAND. Too good—far too good for such a foolish man as me.

ARAMINTA. None's too good for you, Samuel. I'm properly proud to wed you, and I'll do my very bestest.

(GEORGE *and* PETRONELL *are now seen hand in hand, crossing window.*
HENRY *comes back to* L. *of table.* GEORGE *and* PETRONELL *stand in doorway.*)

HENRY (*down behind table* L.C). Ha, ha! Three weddings in sight, souls—three weddings under one roof; and some pretty eating and drinking for all of us, please God!

(CHURDLES ASH *throws his hat on floor*)

CURTAIN.

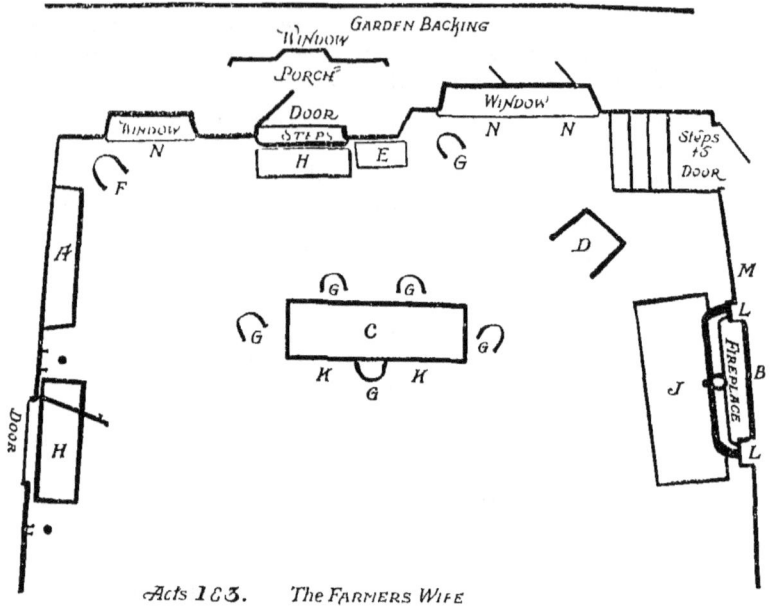

Acts I & 3. *The* FARMERS WIFE

FURNITURE AND PROPERTY PLOT

ACTS I AND III

FURNITURE

A. Oak dresser—shelves and drawers.
B. Kitchen stove in fireplace

C. Large common table.
D. Granny armchair
E. Small table
F. Wheelback armchair
G. 6 wheelback small chairs.
H. 2 black mats
I. Fender
J. Rag hearthrug
K. 2 red hassocks under table
L. Mantelshelf with valance under it.

M. Whip rack above mantelshelf.
N. Curtains on windows
●. 3 hat-pegs on wall—by door down R.
3 hat-pegs above door

PROPERTIES

On Top Shelf.—Copper ornaments, books.
Below—6 blue-and-white plates—mirror 6 small plates, 6 saucers, sugar-basin and spoon Meat dish (to break). Workbasket. 1 blue milk-jug and 1 brown milk-jug and milk. 6 cups on hooks.
Under Dresser.—2 jugs—flour-bin and pan.
In Drawer (1)—Writing-pad and pencil Tin of tobacco and box of matches.
In Drawer (2)—White tablecloth.

Check tablecloth on it
Gun ramrod and rag on it
Black tray on it
Saucepan on stove.

Ornaments, matches, boxes of gums, tobacco-jar, bottle of oil on it.
3 whips on it.
3 flower-pots (geraniums) on each window.
1 small fern pot on sill of porch window.
Pipe for SWEETLAND
Penknife and screw of tobacco for ASH.

Off Stage L—Black coat, blue tie and hair-brush.
Off Stage R—2 rabbits—marrow—book—2 jars of cider (empty).
Big tray with plate of bread and butter, plate of dry bread.
Cake on plate and knife Custard in glass dish, and spoon.
Tea in teapot 6 spoons 6 knives
Box of Fuller's earth, and rag Kettle of hot water.

THE FARMER'S WIFE.

Garden Backing

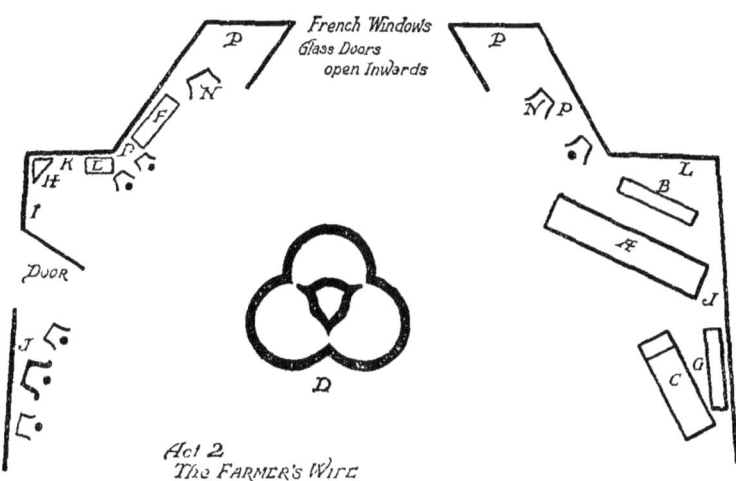

*Act 2
The FARMER'S WIFE*

ACT II

FURNITURE.

A   Large table
    White cloth on it.

PROPERTIES

1 dozen cups, saucers and spoons, 12 plates, 3 milk-jugs, 3 vases of flowers, teapot (tea), hot-water kettle (hot water), coffee urn (coffee), sugar-basin (sugar) Teacloth Taper. Box of matches. 2 plates of cakes 1 dish of cakes Plate of buns and plate of bread-and-butter sandwiches. Glass dish of cream

B   Long form behind table.
C   Sofa L
D   3-seated ottoman.
E   Small table R
F. Small table R C.

G. Side table L.

H   What-not (3 tier) up R
I   Mirror on wall down R
J   Picture on wall L
K   Ship in case R C
L   1 fish in case L C
M   Special portrait in gilt frame R (of Captain Tapper, merchant)
N. 2 gilt chairs R C. and L C.
●. Armchair
    Lady's chair } (R).
    4 small chairs }
    Pedestal and plant R C.
    "Drain Pipe" of rushes, etc., L
P   Lace and plush curtains on gilt rod.
Butler's tray (for props) off stage R
Clothes basket (for props) off stage R.
Off Stage R —Invalid chair
    Tray with 6 ices and spoons on dishes.
    Bowl of plums
    Basket of plums.
    Smelling-salts
    Pile of small plates.
    Pipe and tobacco-box for HENRY.
    Trick line on door R.

Cushion and antimacassar on it
2 cushions and antimacassar on it
Fancy box and bowl of roses on it
Postcard album—framed photo and vase of flowers on it.
2 vases of roses—4 cups and saucers, glass dish of fruit and siphon of soda on tray on it

Vase of flowers and ornaments on it.

{ Antimacassar on it and cushion.
{ Antimacassar on it

PROPERTY PLOT

ACT III

Same as Act I.

Pastry-board, flour-bin, flour-dough, rolling-pin, knife, pie-dish with sliced apples, teacloth. 8 wine glasses and bottle cherry brandy in up-stage dresser cupboard.

Tray on dresser.

Bowl—bucket and saucepan on mat front of wheelback armchair.

Postcard on mantelshelf.

Off Stage R.—2 parcels, 2 portmanteaux, 2 bunches of laurel. Telegram in envelope. 2 shells. Apple.

See white cloth in drawer 2, and gun, marrow, book and jars cleared.

Check tablecloth in drawer 1.

LIGHTING PLOT

ACT I

Float.—Pale blue and pale amber, $\frac{3}{4}$ up.

No. 1 Batten.—Floods—Pale blue and frosts in 2, 3, 4, 5.

Pale pink and frosts in 1, 6 and 4 spots.

No. 3 Batten.—White.

No. 4 Batten.—White and blue.

No. 5 Batten.—Blue.

3 $\frac{1}{2}$-watts light straw on to ground row at back of windows.

1 $\frac{1}{2}$-watt white through porch window.

Arcs.—1 white focus through each window from P. side to O P. side (L. to R).

Bunch light behind each door.

Fire alight.

Amber length under window C.

ACT II

Float.—Pale blue, white, amber and pink, $\frac{3}{4}$ up.

No. 1 Batten.—As Act I.

No. 4 Batten.—As Act I and pale amber.

No 5.—Blue batten fall on to sky cloth.

Bunch light behind door R.

ACT III

Same as Act I.

Batten on and arc lights through windows reversed, viz. from R. to L.

BLUE EYES.

OTHER TITLES AVAILABLE FROM SAMUEL FRENCH

COCKEYED
William Missouri Downs

Comedy / 3m, 1f / Unit Set

Phil, an average nice guy, is madly in love with the beautiful Sophia. The only problem is that she's unaware of his existence. He tries to introduce himself but she looks right through him. When Phil discovers Sophia has a glass eye, he thinks that might be the problem, but soon realizes that she really can't see him. Perhaps he is caught in a philosophical hyperspace or dualistic reality or perhaps beautiful women are just unaware of nice guys. Armed only with a B.A. in philosophy, Phil sets out to prove his existence and win Sophia's heart. This fast moving farce is the winner of the HotCity Theatre's GreenHouse New Play Festival. The St. Louis Post-Dispatch called Cockeyed a clever romantic comedy, Talkin' Broadway called it "hilarious," while Playback Magazine said that it was "fresh and invigorating."

Winner!
of the HotCity Theatre GreenHouse New Play Festival

"Rocking with laughter...hilarious...polished and engaging work draws heavily on the age-old conventions of farce: improbable situations, exaggerated characters, amazing coincidences, absurd misunderstandings, people hiding in closets and barely missing each other as they run in and out of doors...full of comic momentum as Cockeyed hurtles toward its conclusion."
–Talkin' Broadway

SAMUELFRENCH.COM

OTHER TITLES AVAILABLE FROM SAMUEL FRENCH

THE RIVERS AND RAVINES
Heather McDonald

Drama / 9m, 5f / Unit Set
Originally produced to acclaim by Washington D.C.'s famed Arena Stage. This is an engrossing political drama about the contemporary farm crisis in America and its effect on rural communities.

"A haunting and emotionally draining play. A community of farmers and ranchers in a small Colorado town disintegrates under the weight of failure and thwarted ambitions. Most of the farmers, their spouses, children, clergyman, banker and greasy spoon proprietress survive, but it is survival without triumph. This is an *Our Town* for the 80's."
– *The Washington Post*

SAMUELFRENCH.COM

www.ingramcontent.com/pod-product-compliance
Lightning Source LLC
Chambersburg PA
CBHW070645300426
44111CB00013B/2269